Poetry in Motion

Northern Ireland
Edited by Kelly Oliver

First published in Great Britain in 2004 by:
Young Writers
Remus House
Coltsfoot Drive
Peterborough
PE2 9JX
Telephone: 01733 890066
Website: www.youngwriters.co.uk

All Rights Reserved

© *Copyright Contributors 2003*

SB ISBN 1 84460 355 5

Foreword

This year, the Young Writers' 'Poetry In Motion' competition proudly presents a showcase of the best poetic talent selected from over 40,000 up-and-coming writers nationwide.

Young Writers was established in 1991 to promote the reading and writing of poetry within schools and to the youth of today. Our books nurture and inspire confidence in the ability of young writers and provide a snapshot of poems written in schools and at home by budding poets of the future.

The thought effort, imagination and hard work put into each poem impressed us all and the task of selecting poems was a difficult but nevertheless enjoyable experience.

We hope you are as pleased as we are with the final selection and that you and your family continue to be entertained with *Poetry In Motion Northern Ireland* for many years to come.

Contents

Carrickfergus College, Carrickfergus

Daniel Thomas Duong (11)	1
Kristofer Crockard (11)	1
Adam Martin (11)	2
Ronnie McDowell (11)	2
Ashleigh Ward (11)	3
Jenna Pascoe (11)	3
Amy Newell (11)	4
Danielle Tracy Officer (11)	4
Gemma Brown (12)	5
Laura McMaw (12)	5
Rebecca Workman (11)	6
Howard Milliken (11)	6
Julie-ann Galway (11)	7
Rebecca Dickson (12)	7
Kyle McVicker (12)	8
Jill Stewart (11)	9
Janice Hillock (11)	10
Adam Mannis (14)	10
Rachel Campbell (11)	11
Samantha Sinclair (11)	11
Hannah Johnston (11)	12
Stacey Brown (13)	12
Joy Montgomery (11)	13
Andrew Rainey (13)	13
Garry Hamilton (12)	14
Natasha Martin (12)	14
Luke Whitall (11)	15
Colleen Graham (11)	15
Jonathan Sloan (12)	16
Darcy Scott (12)	16
Lee Cassells (11)	17
Emma Herron (12)	17
Nicole Graw (11)	18
Katrina Beggs (12)	19
Andrew David Lutton (11)	20
Adrienne Braden (11)	20
Beccie Bloomfield (11)	21
Conor Houston (11)	21

Zoe McMaster (11)	22
Carolyn Rea (11)	22
David Allen (13)	23
Stephanie Woods (12)	23
Linda Jane Browne (13)	24
Rebecca Beattie (11)	24
Julie-Anne Williams Curran (13)	25
Kirsty McCullough (11)	25
Tanita Gray (11)	26
Keith Weller (11)	26
Melissa Donald (11)	27
Michaela Tutt (12)	27
Morgan Manganelli (12)	28
Michelle Burgess (11)	28
Claire Scott (13)	29
Michael Barnaby (12)	29
Paula McMaw (12)	29
Robert Orr (11)	30
Rebecca Welsh (11)	30
Ashlie Loney (12)	30
Ashton McDermott (11)	31

Carrickfergus Grammar School, Carrickfergus

Edward Thoburn (12)	31
Kirsty McClean (14)	32
Jennifer Donnelly (12)	33
Russell Stockman (11)	33
Emma Harrison (12)	34
Phillip Arthur (13)	34
Peter Johnston (15)	35
Lauren McFarland (13)	35
Daryl Haire (14)	36
Katie McKenzie (12)	37
Stephanie McDermott (15)	38
Stephanie Walker (15)	38
Graham McCracken (14)	39
Kirstie Lammey (12)	39
Tasha Gray (14)	40
Jamie Crates (11)	40
Michelle Martin (14)	41
Nicola Ford (11)	41
Tony Snoddy (12)	42

Lauren Sherwood (14)	43
Jaimie Welsh (12)	44
Karl Love (12)	45
Mark Kernohan (12)	46
Jonathan Ritchie (11)	46
Leanne Ross (12)	47
Jessica Moore (12)	47
Gemma Luney (12)	48
Matthew Shaw (13)	48
Sarah Davis (13)	49
Steven Warden (12)	49
Craig Patterson (12)	50
David McClenaghan (11)	50

Fort Hill College, Lisburn

Francine Harper (13)	51
Justine Crossey (12)	51
Brian Ross (12)	52
Matthew Murdoch (13)	52
Marc Simpson (12)	53
Shannon Bagnall (11)	53
Phil McKibben (12)	54
Nicola Hunt (11)	54
Lee-Ann Graham (12)	55
Terry Mairs (13)	55
Susan McKnight (13)	56
Alex Gibson (11)	56
Terri Houston (12)	57
Matthew Briggs (11)	57
Kathy Moore (11)	58
Rachael McCready (12)	58
Nicole Edmonds (11)	59
Melissa Thompson (11)	59
Samantha Coyle (12)	60
Nathan Donald (11)	60
Nathan Loughead (12)	61
Catherine Mercer (11)	61
Daryl Connery (11)	61
Caaron Garrett (11)	62
Trudi McCourt (11)	62
Tiffany McAllister (12)	63
Jordon Foster (11)	63

Christopher Hull (12)	64
Philip Kinghan (11)	64
Diane Carlisle (13)	65
Scott Jacques (12)	65
Ashlea Thompson (12)	66
Emma Ferguson (11)	66
Megan Archer (12)	67
Kiera Reid (11)	67
Jenna Hannigan (12)	68
Dean Rainey (11)	68
Kelly Stewart (11)	69
Alana McGahey (12)	69
Karl McCready (13)	70
Sophie Williamson (12)	70
Victoria Stuart (12)	71
Leanne Nelson (13)	71
Zara Diamond (11)	72
Nathan Stephens (12)	72
Becky Lee (11)	73
Jasmine Gillett (11)	73
Kirsty Scott (11)	74
Rachel Hayes (11)	74
Andrew Agnew (11)	74
Lyndsey Smyth (12)	75
David Gregg (11)	75
Sheryl White (12)	76
Sarah Maxwell (11)	76
Ethan Megrath (12)	77
Neil Irwin (11)	77
Aimée Harbinson (12)	78
Conor McCahon (11)	78
Andrew Maye (11)	79

Loreto Grammar School, Omagh

Kerry-Ann McMackin (13)	79
Grainne McGread (13)	80
Lauren Harper (11)	80
Verity Mayers (14)	81
Fionnuala Hinds (15)	81
Charlene McCarron (14)	82

Methodist College, Belfast

Rebecca Andrews (12)	82
Amy Stubbings (16)	83
Mark Elliott (15)	83
Philip Smyth (12)	84
Niall Annett (12)	84
Robert Coburn (16)	85
Lisa McKim (13)	85
Debi Moore (17)	86
Anna Coburn (12)	87
Hannah Wilson (14)	88
Julia McClure (12)	88
Louise Magee (13)	89
Ashleigh Craig (15)	89
Ryan Maxwell (12)	90
Vanessa Cotter (13)	90
Hannah Strudley (15)	91
Clare Mackey (12)	91
Aron Hamilton (12)	92
Luke Acheson (13)	92
Karishma Kusurkar (15)	93
David Martin (12)	93
Sophia McKeever (12)	94
Ryan Deane (16)	95
Colin Kirkpatrick (15)	96
Megan Lynn (12)	97
Andrew Gerard (15)	98
Chuan Hong (16)	98
Colin Williamson (15)	99
Gareth Reilly (11)	99
Nicola Wright (12)	100
Katherine Ross (15)	100
Hannah Litvack (15)	101
Rachel Finlay (15)	101
Kirsty McDonald (15)	102
Sharon Ross (15)	103
Catherine Dugan	104
Karl Irwin (15)	104
Thomas Olver (11)	105
Finola Austin (12)	106
Michael Boyle (12)	107

Maeve Middleton (12)	108
Holly Collins (11)	108
Christian Douglas (12)	109
Aimee Muirhead (12)	109
Juliet Stirling (12)	110
Jonathan Tripathy (15)	111
Chris Carson (12)	112
Brajith Srigengan (12)	112
Heather Murphy (16)	113
Fiona Mulvenna (16)	113
Ben Crothers (16)	114
Eoghan Lavery (16)	114
Antonia McAlister (11)	115
Lynn Hutchinson (16)	116

Omagh Academy, Omagh

Julie Forbes (11)	116
Johanna Neary (14)	117
Christine Scott (15)	117
Zarah-Jayne Muldoon (11)	118
Naomi Deazley (13)	118
Alexandrina Todd (12)	119
Emma Cummings (12)	120
James Riddell (11)	120
Naomi Browne (11)	121
Rachel Leary (11)	121
Beverley Keys (15)	122
John FitzGerald (11)	122
Cara McCarthy (14)	123
Vikki Lyttle (14)	123
Fional Crawford (15)	124
Laura Fleming (15)	125
Lauren Alexander (13)	126
Alistair Barker (12)	126
John Porter (12)	127
Danny Millar (13)	127
Philip Hutchinson (12)	128
Nikita Edgar (11)	128
Jessica Keys (12)	129
David Fulton (14)	129
Rachel Giles (12)	130

Christopher McAuley (13)	130
Richard Vaughan (15)	131
Susan Wilson	131
Alexandra Sproule (11)	132

Omagh High School, Omagh
Robert Giles (14)	132

St Joseph's High School, Omagh
Daniel McGaughey (13)	133
Anne-Marie Devine (11)	134
Amanda Hood (11)	135
Ciaran Browne (11)	136

St Patrick's Academy, Dungannon
Ciara Campbell (11)	137
Megan Kelly (11)	138
Roseanna Weech (11)	139
Tara Mullin (14)	140
Breda O'Kane (15)	141
Catherine Wylie (15)	142

Sacred Heart College, Omagh
Clare Martin (13)	142
Eliza Harvey (12)	143
Sabrina McKenna (13)	143
Aáron Grugan (13)	144
Mark Garrity (13)	145
Cathy Davis (12)	146
Taylor Lowe (12)	146
Daniel Gorman (12)	147
Lauren McCarron (13)	148
Kerrianne Clarke (13)	148
Karen McMahon (13)	149
Barry Kerrigan (13)	149
Aisling McAleer (13)	150
James Keenan (12)	151
Dearbhla Byrne (14)	152
Emma McCullagh (12)	152
Matthew McKenna (12)	153
Aine Morris (15)	153
Maeve Brogan (12)	154

Joanne McGoldrick (12)	154
Conor Rafferty (13)	155
Kieran McCullagh (12)	156
Matthew Walsh (13)	156
Rebecca McDonagh (12)	157
Kerrie Sharkey (11)	157
Roisin McGovern (11)	158
Eamie Gormley (12)	158
Ciara Morris	159
Barry McGinn (11)	159
Aisling Dolan (13)	160
Conor Moore (13)	160
Martin McGoldrick (12)	161
Jonathan Browne (13)	161
Cathal McGuire (12)	162
Darren Mullan (13)	162
Hugh Colton (13)	163
Christopher Colton (13)	163
Kieran Colton (15)	164
Orla Clarke (14)	165
Roisin Quinn (14)	166
Laura Garrity (14)	166
Niamh Goodwin (11)	167
Louise Kelly (14)	167
Helena Kirwan (12)	168
Eamonn McGovern (12)	168
Bernadette Nugent (12)	169
Eamonn McMahon (11)	170
Allana McMenamin (12)	171
Gerald McAleer (12)	172
Shane Mullin (14)	172
Ruairi McGinn (13)	173
Aisling Meenagh (12)	173
Shauna Murphy (12)	174
Erin McGuigan (13)	174
Sarah Owens (12)	175
Mairéad Quinn (11)	175
Emma McCarroll (13)	176
Keri-Anne Donnell (11)	176
Christopher Ruddock (12)	177

The Poems

Mr Shakespeare

I am Mr Shakespeare
I pace the stage
One of my greatest
Hits of age.

Is Hamlet and Macbeth
I like to write
About blood and death.

Murderers lurking,
Armies crashing,
Stabbing, hacking,
Skewering, slashing.

Axes and daggers,
Pike and Claymore
This is what
The public pay for.

They are also fond
Of booing and hissing
And they also like a
Bit of slobbery kissing.

Daniel Thomas Duong (11)
Carrickfergus College, Carrickfergus

Poem About My Dog

I have a dog called Molly
I found her in the street
Her coat is nice and glossy
And also black as peat.
Molly's favourite game is ball,
I throw and kick it against the wall.
Molly digs in the dirt
To see what she can see
It doesn't matter what she finds
She brings it straight to me.

Kristofer Crockard (11)
Carrickfergus College, Carrickfergus

The Lie

The sun shines upon my face,
Taking away all my disgrace,
For I have lied to my mum
Told her things I should have never done.

School to me is just for fun
'Listen and learn!' shouts my mum,
'When you grow up you want a good job,'
How can I tell her, I'm just a slob?

Ten years later here I am,
Standing in a dole queue,
Nobody giving a damn,
How I wish I'd listen to my mum,
Now I know school wasn't just for fun.

Adam Martin (11)
Carrickfergus College, Carrickfergus

Sport

S is for soccer, it is a good game
to score a goal, I really did aim.

P is for pool, like it or not, chalk
up the cue and pocket the lot.

O is for orange, I need to drink to play these
games without a fight.

R is for referee, you must be fit to chase
the boys around the football field.

T is for tennis with racket and ball
come on boys, it's 15-all.

Ronnie McDowell (11)
Carrickfergus College, Carrickfergus

School

School's the place I like to be
With lots to learn and plenty to see.

My favourite classes would have to be
Maths, history, music and IT.

The teachers make learning fun
And in PE we get to run.

We also learn to respect each other
So that we all can get along together.

Rules are needed to keep us safe
And to make school a happy place.

In class I must try my best
To get good marks in my test.

Ashleigh Ward (11)
Carrickfergus College, Carrickfergus

The Great Old Tree

I'd try to reach the tree so tall
But little me was far too small
Climbing him was not allowed
If we could, we'd touch the clouds.

This great old tree, he was our friend
We'd watch him sway and even bend
Then the men to cut him came
Our garden just won't be the same.

The tree's now gone, and we're all sad
The root and bark had all gone bad
Happy thoughts still do remain
We could plant a tree again.

Jenna Pascoe (11)
Carrickfergus College, Carrickfergus

If I Could Fly

If I could fly
I'd go so high I'd touch the clouds
I would let the breeze blow through my hair.

If I could fly
I would taste the sun
As hot as a curry.

If I could fly
I would breath deep and sniff
The scent of the rainbows.

If I could fly
I'd look down at the people on Earth
They would look like ants.

If I could fly
I would dream of flying with birds
And flying to another country in the winter.

If I could fly.

Amy Newell (11)
Carrickfergus College, Carrickfergus

The Girl

There once was a girl who lived in a house
She was tall but a little bit small
She was a kind little girl
She was sometimes bad to her dad
But that was all, she loved her mum
Because she thought she was fun,
She got a cat and called it Pat
She loved watching TV
But she didn't like tidying her room
Because it was always messy, not a bit tidy,
She called for her friends to go for a walk,
Because she really loved to talk.

Danielle Tracy Officer (11)
Carrickfergus College, Carrickfergus

My Secret Place

There is a secret place
Within my heart
And not so far away
And I can hear the wonders
Crash around my ears
As I dream of my secret place.

This special place
Holds many secrets
Deep down in my soul
And makes me *feel*
A special peace
That only I can reach.

So when I'm low
And feeling blue
And need a little lift
I close my eyes
Open my mind
And to my secret place I drift.

Gemma Brown (12)
Carrickfergus College, Carrickfergus

The Weather And Seasons

The rain is a pain tapping on my window
Frame, I always wonder who to blame.

In the winter it's time for gloves and
Scarves, it's so cold that we sit beside our
Fire hearths.

When it's windy, I'm very cold, that's when
I'm told, wrap up in warm clothes and
Cover
My toes.

Laura McMaw (12)
Carrickfergus College, Carrickfergus

Sports

Football is the best,
Nothing can ever beat it,
Running about with a ball at your feet,
Trying to beat the keeper with a good strike.

Basketball is fun to play,
Passing the ball to a player in your team,
Dribbling the ball around the other team,
Trying to win the game.

Rugby is a rough game to play,
Running in head first trying to get the ball,
Head down running with the ball,
Ready to score a try.

Swimming is a really fun game,
Diving and splashing is really fun,
Up and down the pool you go,
Going as fast as you can.

I think sports are really fun ,
I love to play all these sports,
They are really good,
I play them all the time.

Rebecca Workman (11)
Carrickfergus College, Carrickfergus

Birds' Nests

The skylarks nest among the grass
And waving corn is found
The robins on a shady bank
With oak leaves strewn around.

The wren builds in an ivied thorn
Or old and ruined wall
The mossy nest so covered in
You scarce can see it at all.

Howard Milliken (11)
Carrickfergus College, Carrickfergus

Seasons

Autumn
Autumn leaves are crisp and dry
Along the paths they fall and die.

Winter
Winter chill is in the air
Sometimes the cold is hard to bear
Snow, frost and rain are all to blame,
But not to worry, Christmas will soon be here again.

Spring
Spring is a lovely time of year
Everything is growing back again
Flowers are budding, birds are singing
It's a wonderful, magical time of year.

Summer
Summer sun is here again
Say goodbye to the rain,
Nights are light and full of cheer,
Parties and fun for the rest of the year.

Julie-ann Galway (11)
Carrickfergus College, Carrickfergus

School!

Monday morning comes so fast,
Now it's time for my first class,
My favourite, English! Hip, hip, hooray,
Next one's Geog, well what can I say?
Oh well, I'm sure it will be fun,
Next it's break, so it's time to run.
I never knew school could be so great,
Meet lots of new people and my new best mate,
The bell has rung, now time to go home,
Along the corridor we all roam,
See you tomorrow, we all shout
And that's what school is all about!

Rebecca Dickson (12)
Carrickfergus College, Carrickfergus

Pets

Animals are great, I like them all
The fat and the skinny
The short and the tall.

My cat is the best
She likes hunting for rats
But when she can't find them
She's not very happy
And often she will turn to be very snappy.

Next is my hamster
Who is really quite small
So that is why we let him run in a ball.

Then there's our budgie
He squawks quite a lot
We really wouldn't mind
If he would learn how to talk.

Last of all we have different fish
And the cats seem to think
They would make a tasty dish.

The goldfish are huge
Getting bigger and bigger
We just hope we don't
Get them served for our dinner.

Kyle McVicker (12)
Carrickfergus College, Carrickfergus

My Pet Poem

In through the castle, shiny and bright,
Out under the arch, like a whippet in flight,
That's our Sparkle the fish, he shines like a star in the night.

Smooth and white, with a long sweeping tail,
Blue eyes so bright, with a lavender spot above the beak,
Our acrobat swings, from perch to perch,
Around 360º and a somersault land, that's
                our Snowy the budgie so grand.

Sable and white, so old, but so bright,
Four bendy wee legs, a tiny wee tail,
She's only six inches, but oh what a ball,
Tilly our dog, is as mad as a hatter,
Treats galore and eats no matter.

Three cream balls of fluff, with tiny brown ears,
Three little brown noses, with whiskers to match,
They hop to and fro, nibbling at dandelions,
Sleeping so much, Coco, Fluffy and Flo,
Our three baby bunnies, who are going to grow.

Our two superstars, Tute and Jack,
Win us ribbons and trophies to our delight,
They are grey and chestnut, with breeding so great,
Our show ponies we love, they are truly first rate.

Jill Stewart (11)
Carrickfergus College, Carrickfergus

Seasons

Autumn
Watch all the leaves turn yellow, brown and red,
Watch all the flowers going dead.
Listen to the raindrops falling to the ground,
Feel the cold spreading all around.

Winter
Watch all the children playing in the snow,
Listen to the strong winds blow.
Wrap up warm to go out and play,
Red noses at the end of the day.

Spring
Watch all the leaves growing back on the trees,
Listen to the sounds of buzzing bees.
Watch all the daisies growing in the grass,
Listen to the birds flying past

Summer
See the sun creeping through the window early in the morning,
Watch all the flowers growing without warning.
Eat ice cream with all of your friends,
Wear shorts and T-shirts until the summer ends.

Janice Hillock (11)
Carrickfergus College, Carrickfergus

Space

Space is black
Like a night sky
The stars glow
Like a lighthouse in the yonder,
The moon is as bright
As a torch light shining
Through a dark forest
Beaming through the trees.

Adam Mannis (14)
Carrickfergus College, Carrickfergus

School

I wake up in the morning at ten-past eight
Get ready quickly so I'm not late
Uniform on
Breakfast all gone
So I had better hurry along.

Three hours later half the day's over
Geography, English, history and science
Maps and writing and learning the past
Experiments on particles and dreadful maths!

We've RE and PE and HE and SE
And Spanish and music and games and IT
Technology, library, art and design
Loads to do until three twenty-five.

Now it's last class, can't wait for the bell
The bell's just rung and . . . everyone's gone.

Rachel Campbell (11)
Carrickfergus College, Carrickfergus

My Holiday In Spain

In August my family and I went to Spain
And I was certain it would not rain
It was really warm so I went into the pool
And when I got in, it was lovely and cool.

In the water my sister and I played ball
Sometimes I would catch it and sometimes I would fall,
When I got tired, I would lie in the sun
Then we would go and have some fun.

At night we danced with the reps
And they would teach us some fancy steps
All the fun was really great
But it was time for bed as it was getting late.

Samantha Sinclair (11)
Carrickfergus College, Carrickfergus

School

I hate school
For it is so not cool
You sit on a stool
And work like a fool.

I am always glad
When the last bell goes
I jump off my chair
Like I just don't care.

I walk to the station
With all of my friends
I get on my train
But it then starts to rain.

I get off at my stop
And I'm glad to get home
I kick off my shoes
And have a short snooze.

Hannah Johnston (11)
Carrickfergus College, Carrickfergus

Best Friends

My best friends are so much fun,
I love them very much,
Our friendship will always last
And not go by us fast.
They are very precious to me,
They always will be,
We like to hang about our streets
And listen to our beats,
We make up our bands
And sell them to our fans,
We fling our hair round and round,
Until we fall upon the ground,
They make me laugh and make me cry,
They'll be my friends until *we* die!

Stacey Brown (13)
Carrickfergus College, Carrickfergus

Seasons Of Colour

I love to see the world change colour,
From autumn, winter, spring and summer.
The trees are alive, the leaves are dead,
New roots spring up from all their beds.

The summer sun lights up the sky,
In autumn leaves fall off and die.
The winter sees the animals sleep,
But springtime wakes and the little lambs leap.

Autumn colours red and gold,
Winter white and very cold.
Springtime blossoms pink and green,
Summer days with strawberries and cream.

So when you look at the world outside,
Do remember to keep your eyes open wide.
Think of the colours we can see each day
And how they change along the way.

Joy Montgomery (11)
Carrickfergus College, Carrickfergus

Rockets

Rockets come in different shapes and sizes!
Rockets give a loud and low *bang!*
Rockets are very dangerous and you
Can get seriously hurt!
Rockets give out big bright colours in the sky!
Rockets have different names like
Air bombs and Catherine wheels!
Rockets are not allowed to be
Sold to children under 18 years of age!

Andrew Rainey (13)
Carrickfergus College, Carrickfergus

My Football Fever Poem

The World Cup final's here
The crowd assembled cheer
The anthems play
On this fine day
Supporters filled with fear.

The whistle starts the game
The team so full of fame
Sven's fingers are crossed
He thinks we've lost
Each player much the same.

The final minutes run
The pitch alight with sun
It's still nil-nil
But score we will
Before the end has come.

The ball is up their end
So Beckham kicks a bend
Cole heads it in
Bangs heads with Finn
And celebrates their win!

Garry Hamilton (12)
Carrickfergus College, Carrickfergus

My Cat Does My Homework

My cat does my homework
At home every night
He answers each questions
And get them all right.

There's only one problem
With homework with Clover
I cannot turn in work
That's been slobbered all over.

Natasha Martin (12)
Carrickfergus College, Carrickfergus

Autumn's Here

Autumn's here, autumn's here
The summer has passed
The autumn is here.

The birds have flown
The sky is clear
The leaves lie all around us
Little creatures build their nests
Ready for hibernation.

The golden crisp leaves
Fall to the ground
So gently they fall
With no sound at all
Burnt orange
Golden yellow
And rusty red
Lying on the ground
Like a thick leafy bed.

Autumn's here, autumn's here
The summer has passed
The autumn is here.

Luke Whitall (11)
Carrickfergus College, Carrickfergus

My Dog Jack

My dog Jack is a boxer
He boxes all day and night
My dog Jack is a boxer
He can give you a terrible fright
My dog Jack is a boxer
I wonder what kind he is
Is he a small one, is he a big one
No - he's just a normal little Jack.

Colleen Graham (11)
Carrickfergus College, Carrickfergus

My Cat

I have a cat called Lucy
And I love her so
We have had her since a baby
And I watched her grow and grow.

She likes to play with balls
And likes to jump off walls
She's a wee bit mad
But she's the best cat I've ever had.

She always baths herself
As she doesn't like soapy bubbles
And when she's nice and clean
I give her lots of cuddles.

My mum always shouts at her
As she's always under her feet
So I scoop her up and lie her down
And she falls fast asleep.

Jonathan Sloan (12)
Carrickfergus College, Carrickfergus

Colourful Autumn

Crimson, golden and russet
Red, orange and brown.
All of them migrate to the ground,
Swirling and spinning,
Twisting and turning
And finally they touch the ground.

Gracefully they fall to the ground,
We walk on them *crunch, crunch,*
As they die away, we see more fall
And as we see the colours
We think of colourful autumn.

Darcy Scott (12)
Carrickfergus College, Carrickfergus

Winter

As I look out my window I see snow fall,
Then something catches my eye, it's an icicle hanging,
From my wall.
Again it is this time of year when I like
Watching snow falling on my windowpane.

Some kids are playing outside, they're having lots of fun,
As I watch this one boy
He keeps throwing snowballs
At someone, then they throw one back.

I put my coat and hat on and just as I
Walk out to the porch, I hit the floor as a boy
Throws a snowball at my door. I get back up
And throw snowballs as he runs.

We all are playing snowball fights
This lasts for a while until somebody
Shouts, 'Goodbye Lee I'm away home for my tea.'

Lee Cassells (11)
Carrickfergus College, Carrickfergus

The Summer

P7 ended with a blast,
It was a hard year, but it went so fast,
I said goodbye to all my primary school friends
It was as if that part of my life had come to an end.

The rest of the summer was spent back at home
And I was always using the phone,
My new school was almost ahead
On the 29th of August, my new school was beaming
In my head.

Emma Herron (12)
Carrickfergus College, Carrickfergus

A Night To Remember

I was walking down the street
Late one night
I saw something strange
It was shining very bright.

I ran to the door
For someone to tell
There was no knocker
So I rang the bell.

She answered the door
All covered in flour
She said 'Who's outside
At this late hour?'

I tried to tell the lady
Just what I'd seen,
She said 'My dear child
Where have you been?'

'I was taking a shortcut
Across your back
And I saw something shine
In your old shack.'

Out from the shadows
A figure did appear
It was Mrs Jones' husband
He'd been on the beer.

Nicole Graw (11)
Carrickfergus College, Carrickfergus

Rain

Rain is really boring,
You're always stuck inside,
It makes me feel like snoring,
I like snuggling up on the settee,
I wonder what it's doing outside,
It makes me eager to see.

I look outside, it's dull and grey,
It makes me feel so down,
Then I begin to wish, it was back to May,
I remember it all being sunny,
I wish it was,
But instead my nose is all runny.

It makes me smile to remember,
I love Christmas,
But it's ages until December,
I love snow, not rain,
I love it when it snows,
As you don't have to suffer any pain.

I look outside, the rain's away,
I put on my shoes,
To go out and play
And dry, I hope it will stay,
So there's me happy,
Until another day.

Katrina Beggs (12)
Carrickfergus College, Carrickfergus

Transport

Bikes so yellow, black and green,
The fastest things, I've ever seen,
Engines loud and lights so bright,
Quick as a flash, they're out of sight.

The planes take off, again and again,
The announcement calls, 'Go to gate 10,'
The excitement rises as people make way
To the start of their holidays to
Lands far away.

Patiently, patiently, we wait for the ship,
Car after car, in queues tightly knit,
Not before long the man waves us on,
Ready to sail with the harbour long gone.

Clickety clack, down the track they go,
Fast and slow, fast and slow,
Passing each station on their way
Home, home after another day.

But I'll tell you the best way, oh yes by far
Is to sit in a big fancy car
With me at the wheel driving so keen,
All I need is to be seventeen!

Andrew David Lutton (11)
Carrickfergus College, Carrickfergus

Ellie

There was a young girl called Ellie,
Who wanted too much telly,
Then her eyes turned square
And she looked like a hare,
Then wobbled like a piece of jelly.

Adrienne Braden (11)
Carrickfergus College, Carrickfergus

Seasons

As I sit with a poem to write,
I look upon the berries bright,
As autumn comes and summer ends,
The leaves are red and yellow blends.

The frost upon my fingers bites,
It's long and cold, the winter night
Young children play out in the snow,
While trees avoid their north wind foe.

As nights get short, the days get long,
I listen out for the blackbird's song,
As grass turns green and buds appear,
The yellow of spring bulbs give cheer.

As the days start to get lighter,
All the garden starts to get brighter,
As the colours begin to flow
Trees, their berries begin to grow.

Beccie Bloomfield (11)
Carrickfergus College, Carrickfergus

The Green Pill

I went to the doctor because I was ill
So he prescribed me a daily *green* pill.

I went to the chemist who gave me it quick
Because he could see I was about to be sick.

I took the *green* pill but it did me no good
And even it put me off eating my food.

I returned to the doctor the following day
What a shock when I saw on the floor he did lay.

I looked down at his pale face and quietly said -
'Oh doctor, the *green* pill is now yours instead!'

Conor Houston (11)
Carrickfergus College, Carrickfergus

Autumn

Autumn time has come,
Kicking leaves is fun,
Red, green, orange, yellow and brown,
Lying on the frosty ground.

31st of October,
Coming a little closer,
Crunchy apples, dainty pears,
Apple tarts selling in pairs.
Fireworks going *crackle, pop, bang,*
All I can hear is *bang, bang, bang.*

Frosty days and frosty nights,
Sick and homeless, shivering at night,
Not even having a bite of
Crunchy apples, dainty pears,
All those tarts selling in pairs.

Zoe McMaster (11)
Carrickfergus College, Carrickfergus

Waking Up To Winter

As I look through my window,
What do I see? Winter staring back at me.
The glittering snowflakes gently falling down
And children making snowmen as round as can be.

The trees have shed their leaves as fast as can be,
As I look through my window,
What do I see? Winter staring back at me.

See children sliding around and up and down,
Side to side, always falling down,
As I look through my window,
What do I see? Winter staring back at me.

Carolyn Rea (11)
Carrickfergus College, Carrickfergus

Snow

Snow!
Watch as it hits the ground,
Covering the hills and the trees
Watch it snow.
As it covers the paths and the cars
Watch it snow.
I make snow angels and make snowmen
Watch it snow.
I go playing in the snow sometimes
I kick the snow and have snowball fights
Watch it snow.
As it gets darker it stops
Watch it snow.
My mum tells me to put on gloves and a scarf
Watch it snow.
Now it's nearly time to go
So I'll play in the snow
I start to make angels
Watch it snow.

David Allen (13)
Carrickfergus College, Carrickfergus

School

In English we read books,
In HE my two teachers want us to be cooks.

In maths we do lots and lots of sums,
That's when we all want our mums.

In science we use things like a tripod or a Bunsen burner,
In school I feel like a young learner.

But school has its bad times and good times,
But now I'm thinking of lots of rhymes.

Stephanie Woods (12)
Carrickfergus College, Carrickfergus

Purple Is My Favourite Colour

Purple is my favourite colour
It's very colourful and *bright*
There's purple in the rainbow
Sometimes in flying kites.

Face from white to purple
When one is in a rage
Wrinkly hands this colour
When we suffer from old age.

My bedroom's coloured purple
Drawers and wardrobe too
The colour makes me happy
When I am feeling blue.

Everyone likes different colours
Some like red, blue or green
But purple is the one for me
I even see it in my dream.

Linda Jane Browne (13)
Carrickfergus College, Carrickfergus

My Teddy Bear!

I love you though you're old and worn,
I've had you since the day I was born.

Your little eyes still twinkle like stars,
I've played with you for hours and hours.

I love your little ears and toes,
Your little pink and funny nose.

You still have a lovely smile,
I think I'll keep you for a while.

You live with me in my bed,
You are my favourite super ted.

Rebecca Beattie (11)
Carrickfergus College, Carrickfergus

My House

My house is in the Crescent,
It's white and brown and pleasant,
On the door is number seven,
Enter in no later than eleven.

As you enter in the hall,
My dad will give a call,
Hands washed, stop your looking,
Mum's in the kitchen cooking.

My room is in the attic,
Where I can be a TV fanatic,
It's pink and green and really mean,
With all my Buffy posters.

Julie-Anne Williams Curran (13)
Carrickfergus College, Carrickfergus

How Long To Christmas?

October, October, the month of the year
When Christmas time is getting near,
Adults are hassled, they think of the bills,
While children look at Argos books and are really thrilled.

November, November, the shops are so busy,
Employees are running around in a tizzy,
But if you're a shopper and wanting to pay,
Hope you're not in a hurry because you'll be there all day.

December, December, the countdown is on,
How long will it be until Christmas Day dawn?
Don't forget about others, we want to care
And what better way to do it - *than to share.*

Kirsty McCullough (11)
Carrickfergus College, Carrickfergus

Winter Morning

As I awake in my bed
I hear the children playing happily outside,
I pull the curtains back
And watch them having snow fights.
It is cold and frosty,
Their faces are rosy red,
They're wrapped up warm against
The freezing cold.
Children laughing gleefully as they
Throw snowballs at each other.
Others making snow angels in the
Sparkling white snow,
They say goodbye to each other
Because it's time to go.

Tanita Gray (11)
Carrickfergus College, Carrickfergus

My Hamster

Nibbles, Nibbles chewing his cage,
He really is full of rage.
He is always trying to get out,
Because if he doesn't he will shout.

He likes to roll around the hall
In his round, plastic ball,
I like to give him stuff to chew
And I keep his cage as good as new.

I like to handle him in my hand
And he really does think it's grand,
Nibbles is my delight,
Except when he rattles his cage, most of the night.

Keith Weller (11)
Carrickfergus College, Carrickfergus

A Graceful Autumn

Leaves falling slowly
Twisting, twirling and floating
Golden, yellow, orange and brown
Brightly falling from the sky.

A prickly, spiky hedgehog
Getting food ready
For a long deep sleep.

Clothes are warm, cosy,
Nice, cuddly and dry
Gloves keep my hands warm
In case they get frostbite.

Conkers falling on the
Wet ground, spiky covering
Which hurts your hands.

The wind howling,
Lifting up the leaves,
Crunch, crunch
As your feet stand on the leaves.

Melissa Donald (11)
Carrickfergus College, Carrickfergus

Friendship Poem

F orever friends
R eally good friends
I always go shopping for my friends
E very day we speak to each other
N ever break up
D ifferent friend every day
S hare all our secrets together
H ave fun every day
I enjoy everything we do together
P enpals forever.

Michaela Tutt (12)
Carrickfergus College, Carrickfergus

My Holidays

When I swim in the tropical ocean,
I always put on lots of lotion,
Always sitting in the sun
Always playing and having fun.

Always shopping in the city,
Sometimes looking very pretty,
Always sitting by the pool,
Always trying to keep cool.

Sometimes I get a smoothy,
On the boat I feel woozy,
Never want to go home
But I'm missing the dog and its bone.

Missing my mum and the brothers,
Missing my friends and their mothers,
Looking around me and at the sun,
Maybe I can laugh and not miss my mum.

Morgan Manganelli (12)
Carrickfergus College, Carrickfergus

My First Day At School

As I get off the bus
I am starting to make a fuss
I feel like a fish on a hook
I hope I remembered all of my books
As I walk the long way
I am beginning to sway
Please don't let me fall on the way
As I walk in the door, I begin to shake
Please hurry up and let it be break
The final bell rings
And I begin to sing
Now I can catch the bus
Without any fuss.

Michelle Burgess (11)
Carrickfergus College, Carrickfergus

Teachers

T eachers are nice
E very so often they shout
A nd sometimes they get angry
C lasses are sometimes funny
H ave fun learning at school
E veryone is good at something's like,
R E, French, English, maths,
S chool is good fun, so enjoy it.

Claire Scott (13)
Carrickfergus College, Carrickfergus

My Nickname

B is for beautiful,
A is for argumentative,
R is for rich and famous,
N is for naughty devil,
E is for extra special,
Y is for young and special.

Michael Barnaby (12)
Carrickfergus College, Carrickfergus

Autumn

In autumn the leaves are golden brown,
When they fall, they float to the ground
And when I walk they *crackle* and *crunch,*
They remind me of my breakfast when I munch.
There are roads and tons of leaves about,
You could even call the trees a little lout,
When the autumn is nearly over, the trees are bare,
So I advise them to get clothes to wear.

Paula McMaw (12)
Carrickfergus College, Carrickfergus

A Good Day

A happy day
Is good to keep,
So take it to bed
And put it to sleep.

But when you wake up,
Do not shout,
For a happy day
Will be in doubt.

Robert Orr (11)
Carrickfergus College, Carrickfergus

My Pet Hamster

Hamsters are friendly,
Hamsters are fun,
Mine's a friendly
Harmless one,
Hamsters are cuddly,
Hamsters are cool,
I would not dream of
Taking mine to school.

Rebecca Welsh (11)
Carrickfergus College, Carrickfergus

Winter

Winter days are long and dark,
Leaves are falling in the park.
Wind and rain is all around,
Snow is lying on the ground.

People rushing in and out,
No one wants to hang about,
Sun sets early dark from noon,
Christmas time is coming soon.

Ashlie Loney (12)
Carrickfergus College, Carrickfergus

The Beautiful Game

Football is a jewel
But it really can be cruel,
When you lose the cup by a goal,
You wanna smash a bowl!

When your team score,
You really want more,
But when the keeper lets one in,
You really wanna kick a bin!

When your team is playing bad,
You wanna pass like my dad,
When you pass like my dad,
You know you yourself
You can't be playing bad!

Ashton McDermott (11)
Carrickfergus College, Carrickfergus

Dangers Of Fire

D angerously hot
A nd very wild
N ot to be messed with or
G rannies get riled
E ngulfing flames could
R avish the land
S moke black and thick.

O ver mountains grand
F umes of petrol catching

F ire turning to mayhem it just keeps spreading
I n control of the fire the
R ookies take it, but in the
E nd there's nothing left.

Edward Thoburn (12)
Carrickfergus Grammar School, Carrickfergus

The City Of Life

It is midday and once again the streets are alive with colour,
The colour of excitement and joy, anxiousness and annoyance.
The sounds of cars beeping, humming and roaring past.
The smell of the car fumes and leaking petrol,
Of the faint aroma of baking bread.

As I look around there are so many people,
So many lives taking place.
There is a small child grasping onto his mother's hand
Fearing being caught in the crowd, fearing being lost.
There is an old couple, arm in arm, just wandering slowly,
Not caring where they are going or what is happening around them
Just as long as they are together.

Then there are the business people.
Walking quickly with fixed expressions on their faces.
They have their minds fixed on where they are going,
                                  just walking mindlessly on,
Carrying their briefcases with their lives, possessions, old
                            hopes and dreams stuffed inside,
Not giving a thought to whom they are nudging, pushing
                        down or walking over along the way.

As I sit here in this doorway with newspapers draped over me,
I just think to myself, *who would I be?*
Would I be like the little child, holding on to everything I hold dear,
fearing getting lost or would I be like the old couple?
Would I find the love of my life who would stay by my side,
hold me up, keep me going?
I just hope I wouldn't be like the businessmen,
On my own, holding onto meaningless things such as
money and my pride, stashing all my hopes, dreams and
faith into a briefcase.
You see, I do not have anything in this world
Apart from my faith and these dirt-encrusted clothes.
To lose faith, to me, would be like losing life itself.

Kirsty McClean (14)
Carrickfergus Grammar School, Carrickfergus

Snowy Days

One day I looked out and saw
A big white blanket covering my town
With it getting bigger as each little feather fell onto it
The town once full of hustle and bustle
The streets once busy with cheer
Were now both clean and clear.

The path untouched
Clouds covering the sky
Today the sun seemed rather shy
Later on kids will play
And hit each other while they say
'Heads up' or 'hooray'.

Slowly but surely it fades away
I see some green needle heads
Pricking their way towards the sky
The kids they groan,
Now it's the adults turn to play
While this time they say, 'Hooray!'

Now the town is busy again
And the streets are full of pollution and litter
The rooftops are dark and dirty once more
Until the next time we get that guest
We'll all wait with memories of that fine day.

Jennifer Donnelly (12)
Carrickfergus Grammar School, Carrickfergus

How A Good Monkey Is Shaped

A head like a football,
A neck straight and tall,
A nose wet and soggy,
A mouth that says it all,
An ear like a radar on the side of his head,
A body like my dad's, all hairy and sad.

Russell Stockman (11)
Carrickfergus Grammar School, Carrickfergus

Alone

Alone she sits
Afraid but free
She wonders
Won't you come to rescue me?

There she sits
Wondering why
Won't you come to say goodbye?

Is it true?
Is she gone?
This she wonders
Crying on.

She looked upon her mother's face
Remembering her loving grace
You'll never know what you'll miss
Until it's gone, the end, that's it.

Emma Harrison (12)
Carrickfergus Grammar School, Carrickfergus

Being Blind

The colours I can never see,
Of plants or flowers
Or a bumblebee.
Or the brightness of a summer's day,
For darkness is with me all the way.
I see by smell and sound and touch,
I've come to rely
On these so much,
I know about the sky and sea,
Someone once explained to me,
Of planes and boats, of birds and fish
To see them all would be *my* wish.

Phillip Arthur (13)
Carrickfergus Grammar School, Carrickfergus

The Cottage

Not far from Lough Erne
Lies a small, remote cottage
My grandmother's cottage
A place alone
My refuge
Reached by a rough, beaten lane
Rickety fences set boundaries.
Scarcely seen through great trees
Three muddy, neglected fields
Thistles, rushes, ditches
Seasonal lushness of fields
Honeysuckle trees create
A mild, soothing scent.
Stars undisturbed
Make it seem sacred.
In the heart of rural Fermanagh
Lies a small, remote cottage.

Peter Johnston (15)
Carrickfergus Grammar School, Carrickfergus

My Mum

My mum's a 'What do you want for dinner?' sort of person
A helpful, loving mum.
She's a 'Have you done your homework?' kind of mum.
She loves a good old gossip.

A 'I'm making a cuppa tea, I take it you want some?'
Kind of woman.
She loves a glass a wine, or two.
She's a 'Do you think I'm made of money?' sort of mum.
But no matter what
I still love my mum, I do.

Lauren McFarland (13)
Carrickfergus Grammar School, Carrickfergus

Sydney

The sun bakes the ground,
Making it crack,
Christmas decorations shine tackily,
In the glare of the afternoon sun.

The sun shimmers gently,
On the lightly breaking waves,
A warm wind meanders in from the sea,
Bringing in a light smell of salt.

Waves lap gently on the sea wall,
Wakes grow from the hordes of harbour boats,
Seagulls glide in slowly,
Squealing and pecking bits of food.

Flags flutter in the wind,
Flying from large brilliant white poles,
The sun gently fades away,
Behind the majestic Harbour Bridge.

The opera house reflects,
The last warm sun rays of the day,
The sun disappears behind the sea
And the bats come out to swoop about.

The cool night begins,
The moon shimmers quietly,
Over the large expanse of the harbour,
All is quiet.

Daryl Haire (14)
Carrickfergus Grammar School, Carrickfergus

Old Age

Old age
Is
My grandad
As wrinkled as washing
Hanging on the line
Drinking coffee all the time
All
Day
Long.

Old age
Is
My grandad
Getting his paper
From the shop
Not much to pay
Passing a mate
On his way.

Old age
Is
My grandad
Putting on his glasses
Checking on the scores
What horse has won?
Today? Wow!
It's a double pay.

Katie McKenzie (12)
Carrickfergus Grammar School, Carrickfergus

The Fairground

The happy sound of contented children
Lingering in the sunshine
With a warm breeze
That made moods soar.

Filled with excited children
Running from every direction
With helium filled balloons
Melodious.

The sweet smell of candyfloss
The beautiful sight of children having fun
The continuos sound of high-pitched laughing
Filling the warm, safe atmosphere.

The sun is just on the point of setting
Leaving a golden glow in the sky as dusk begins to fall
The fairground is ablaze of coloured lights
Twinkling, flashing, sparkling.

Stephanie McDermott (15)
Carrickfergus Grammar School, Carrickfergus

Santa

Heart pounding, eyes awake,
Mind racing, eager to anticipate,
What toys have I got? Had Santa been here?
Had I been a good girl all through the year?
Trying to think of anything bad I might have done,
Why would Santa not want to have come?
Has he eaten his cookie and drunk all his milk?
Has he spilt any of it on his red suit of silk?
Creeping towards my bedroom door,
There was my stocking filled on the floor!
Toys and more toys, what was inside there?
Waking the whole house up, 'Santa has been!'
With all these new toys, I felt like a queen!

Stephanie Walker (15)
Carrickfergus Grammar School, Carrickfergus

My Granda

From morning to night he's working
Planting flowers or cutting grass
With a whistle and a smile
That's my granda.

Always doing something
Cutting hedges, sweeping leaves
Looking forward to tomorrow
That's my granda.

A day never wasted
Watching TV or doing the gardening
Never thinking negatively
That's my granda.

Never looks back, always forward
Singing an ancient song while laughing
Always has something good to say
That's my granda.

Graham McCracken (14)
Carrickfergus Grammar School, Carrickfergus

School

My opinion of school is dire
It's like being trapped in a terrible fire.
The teachers are like the flames
Oh I would rather be doing games.

All these subjects we have to do
I feel like a pot of stew.
Those adults who have put me inside
Seem to do it with so much pride.

But of course I am only joking
The fun I am always poking.
My teachers are the best
Please believe I only jest.

Kirstie Lammey (12)
Carrickfergus Grammar School, Carrickfergus

Loneliness

It's dark, cold and lonely
Where could I be?
There is nobody near
Hello?

I hear voices, but,
From where are they coming?
It suddenly goes quiet, silence,
Hello?

Can anyone see me?
What are they doing?
Do they know I'm here?
Hello?

Chills trickling up and down my spine,
I'm scared, nobody's about,
Will I get jumped on?
Is there anyone to guide me?

Please, take me by the hand,
Lead me out of here,
To somewhere light,
To someone I can talk to,
To someone who will befriend me.

Tasha Gray (14)
Carrickfergus Grammar School, Carrickfergus

How A Good Cat Is Shaped

A head like a tennis ball,
A neck like a spring,
A nose like a button,
A mouth like a Polo mint,
An ear like a piece of Toblerone,
A body like a can.

Jamie Crates (11)
Carrickfergus Grammar School, Carrickfergus

Unconditional Love

You were the apple of my eye,
As you bounced upon my knee.
You should have stayed my little girl,
For all eternity.

I used to tell you tales,
Of how I'd fly you to the moon.
But the bedtime stories were over
And all too soon.

With your tattered, blonde hair
And your very thin frame
You're just a shadow of that little girl
Who now looks in so much pain.

Just like a mouse caught in a trap
And a fly caught in a web
If you don't stop taking those drugs
You will have no future ahead.

You're still my little girl
Even though you're twenty-two
No matter what you've done in your life
I will never stop loving you.

Michelle Martin (14)
Carrickfergus Grammar School, Carrickfergus

How A Good Horse Is Shaped

A head like a marrow,
A neck like a tree trunk,
A nose like a button,
A mouth like a U,
An ear like a cone,
A body like a barrel.

Nicola Ford (11)
Carrickfergus Grammar School, Carrickfergus

The Rally

Handling, control, teamwork
That's what rallies are about
The spoiler is stylish
The gearbox is new
The car is just fun to drive.

The satisfaction of winning
The competition to be the best
The Evo 6 just beats the rest.

The first car is off
The rally has started
The Mitsubishi is up next
Rev up the engine soon they'll be off
Waiting for the signal to go
The driver is ready
The navigator is sorted
The green light is so go! Go! Go!

Around the corner
Through the esses
And now a handbrake turn
The crowds applause
But the navigator has lost his place.

The drive is on his own
Is steering his only guide
No speed acceleration and determination are the key.

The car speeds through the ford
But misses the junction
Brakes but hits a brick wall
The car is wrecked his rally is over
And now next time he knows.

Tony Snoddy (12)
Carrickfergus Grammar School, Carrickfergus

Early Morning

It is early morning and it is the start of spring
The air is warm and you can smell the fresh scent of the new flowers.
I am a tree and sit on the top of the town's local hill,
I have a perfect view of the silent town,
I can tell when it's early morning and when it is late at night.

When it is late at night,
All is silent,
The only sounds you can hear are the sound of the occasional drunk
Walking unsteadily down the street
And the movement of the nocturnal animals,
There is also the occasional car,
But now the time has changed and it is early morning.

In the early morning it is silent,
The town seems deserted,
The townsfolk are still in bed and the sun is starting to rise,
The streets and roads are empty, there is not a soul in sight,
Babies, children and adults are all asleep in their beds,
The only sound you can hear is the occasional chime
                                      of the town's clock.

But now the town is waking up,
The sun has risen,
The babies' scream and cry,
The children run around playing,
The adults go in their cars,
The shops are now open,
The streets and roads are filled with people and cars,
Silence is nowhere to be found.

Lauren Sherwood (14)
Carrickfergus Grammar School, Carrickfergus

The Forest

As I walk in the night, through the dark, damp forest,
The brown mud sludging under my feet,
This is a dare to see if I can cope,
In this mystical yet haunted place.

I can hear the ghosts around me,
Squealing until they frighten me to death.
In the daylight the forest seems calm and cosy
And the squirrels run in the trees.

But at night things change,
As the forest becomes
The home of ghosts and ghouls
And all of the unnatural things.

As fear floods through me,
The wolves howl at the whole blue moon.
The moon provides my only light,
In this nightmare of a place.

I hear footsteps behind me,
I turn around, no one is there.
With the wind howling around me,
I turn around and start walking again.

The wind gets louder,
I still hear footsteps.
I turn around, no one there,
I walk faster, trying to get away.

The footsteps are still behind me,
Getting louder, I start to run,
The wind howling in my face,
The thing behind me moves swiftly.

This monster has me tight in his grip.
I realise that this is the end.
There is silence.
I know that now I will never leave the forest.

My ghost now haunts the forest,
Along with the others,
I will be alone,
Wailing to be set free.

Jaimie Welsh (12)
Carrickfergus Grammar School, Carrickfergus

Old Age

Old age
Is
Grannies
Sour as lime
Sewing things to pass the time
As they develop another wrinkly line
Getting older
By the minute.

Old age
Is
Old gentleman
Hair bright as light
Smart ties on and shoes tied tight,
Sucking things, unable to bite,
Looking
Very daper.

Old age
Is
Residents of homes
Stubborn as old mares
Sitting hunched in chairs
Quiet and without cares
Passing
Time away.

Karl Love (12)
Carrickfergus Grammar School, Carrickfergus

Old Age

Old age
Is
Sitting in the chair all day
Repeating yourself day after day
Knitting a new jumper for Ray
Slowwww
All day.

Old age
Is
Boring
Grey hair getting greyer
Grey day even greyer
Grey jumper for Ray
Old age
Is getting greyer.

Old age
Is
Complaining
Too hot, too cold,
Too tight, too loose
Too big, too small,
Always
Never right.

Mark Kernohan (12)
Carrickfergus Grammar School, Carrickfergus

How A Perfect Elephant Is Shaped

A head like a crash helmet,
A trunk like a hose,
A mouth like a compressor,
An ear like a fan,
A body like a beach ball,
A tail like a fly swatter.

Jonathan Ritchie (11)
Carrickfergus Grammar School, Carrickfergus

Terror In The School

Locked up like criminals,
Fighting against sleep,
Terrorised into doing homework,
Woke up by alarm clocks going *beep, beep.*

Teachers threatening to resign,
If we don't do the work,
Children yawning everywhere,
12 o'clock is starting to lurk.

Finally it's time to eat,
In the over-priced lunch room,
Lunch break is over,
It's time to get back to the gloom.

Everyone is in a panic,
As we all search for a pen,
As another test starts,
Oh no not again!

Now it's time for boring maths,
But the day is nearly at an end,
I'm looking forward to tomorrow,
Because it's the *weekend!*

Leanne Ross (12)
Carrickfergus Grammar School, Carrickfergus

How A Good Owl Is Shaped

A head like a ball,
A neck like a screw,
A nose like a tiny button,
A mouth like a peanut,
An ear like a radar,
A body like a huge teddy bear.

Jessica Moore (12)
Carrickfergus Grammar School, Carrickfergus

Old Age

Old age is being wrinkly,
Having diseases
And sneezes,
Sometimes the mind ceases,
Cared for but mindless.

Old age is being lonely,
Having dentures,
Hoarding treasures,
Even scared to venture,
Out of your home.

Old age is being helpless,
Wearing glasses,
Having bus passes,
All they ask is
Someone to care.

Gemma Luney (12)
Carrickfergus Grammar School, Carrickfergus

Ferrari Enzo

In this car the comfort is astounding,
The interior is red and extremely comfortable,
The colour is red and the endurance is paralysing,
It is flash and class like excitement.

The brakes turn red trying to stop,
The alloys are shiny like enjoyment,
The turbos make a loud noise when revving them,
The horse power is exciting.

The drive of this car is rear wheel drive and driving is difficult,
The engine is red-hot when you stop,
The handling is not so good but on straights it is paralysing,
It is of course a Ferrari Enzo.

Matthew Shaw (13)
Carrickfergus Grammar School, Carrickfergus

Old Age

Old age
Is
Toothless
Women making up rumours,
Walking slowly across the road
With the Zimmer frame
The cats are trapped
In the messy house.

Old age
Is
Sagging skin
Topped off with grey hair
Countless locks on the door
Pills and potions
Taking up the smelly cupboards
Teeth smiling from a glass.

Sarah Davis (13)
Carrickfergus Grammar School, Carrickfergus

The Desert

The nothingness of an open space,
The brainwashing, waterless valleys,
The torturing imprisonment of a sandstorm,
The pain inflicting sand underneath your feet.

The total isolation victimises you,
The sand dunes of torture
Stretch for miles around,
The pain inflicting sand underneath your feet.

The emptiness is imprisoning,
The heat is unmatchable,
The dryness is unbearable,
The pain inflicting sand underneath your feet.

Steven Warden (12)
Carrickfergus Grammar School, Carrickfergus

The Table

When I think about a table I think of school.
Dreading to think of the test marks
The aggravating scratch of a pencil on paper
And the fire of summer exams.

But sometimes I think about the pain
That the table is suffering.
Like the sharp point of a pencil
And the ball of a pen.

The suffocating pain of graffiti
Tippex on its surface
Pen on its sides
And scores on its legs.

Now I think about it more
I wouldn't like to be a table
Getting all that abuse
How about you?

Craig Patterson (12)
Carrickfergus Grammar School, Carrickfergus

How A Good Rhinoceros Is Shaped

A head like a T-rex,
A neck like a stump,
Eyes like two pebbles,
His shoulders like humps,
A tail like a lion,
Four legs like tree trunks,
Ears like two bat wings,
As bald as a monk,
Lips like a fish pout,
A horn like a spike,
Skin like old leather,
This animal I like.

David McClenaghan (11)
Carrickfergus Grammar School, Carrickfergus

Seaside

We walk on the sand,
Splash in the sea,
Then we walk on the green land,
I get an ice cream bought for me.

We make castles on the shore,
The sea is warm, silky and blue,
We all want more,
But we have to go home too.

The sun is beaming warm and bright,
Then the sea starts to heat,
This is so warm and so very light,
We really need something to eat.

We all love the dancing around,
The weather starts to get cold and mild,
Trying to get dried on the ground,
That's what we love about the seaside.

Francine Harper (13)
Fort Hill College, Lisburn

After Summer

Autumn is here, summer's past
Weather's getting colder.
Dark nights coming fast
As the year gets older.

The wind is blowing briskly
The sun's heat starts to fade.
The evenings draw in quickly
We do not need the shade.

Hallowe'en will soon be here
Witches, apples, sugar cane.
Christmas with its good cheer
Another year begins again.

Justine Crossey (12)
Fort Hill College, Lisburn

My Football Team

I play for a local football team
That no one ever beats
We are big and mean and lean
And the coach buys us treats.

The season started slow at first
With not a win in sight
Then the coach demanded an energy burst
And we began to put up a fight.

Our matches were worthy of Match of the Day
With goals in every game
I only wish we got some pay
And some of the national fame.

Our next big game is this weekend
We'll pull out all the stops
The message will be clear we'll send
If the goalie makes no fatal drops.

Brian Ross (12)
Fort Hill College, Lisburn

Annie

My little puppy's fur is as soft as a teddy
After her bath she shakes like the trees
Shaking water off her leaves.

When she gets downstairs
She goes straight into the kitchen chairs
Rubbing her nose just like someone
With a cold.

When I take her for a walk
I watch her like a hawk.
When I take her to go to bed
She sleeps like the peace of the dead.

Matthew Murdoch (13)
Fort Hill College, Lisburn

Under My Bed!

What is under my bed?
It's a cosy place,
For my bear which is named Ted
And don't forget the black shoelace.

But a hiding place it might be
So I can sleep and
Not go down to tea.
But don't forget the elastic band.

Maybe just an apple core,
Like a messy bin
And a dart, what will I score?
And the flute made of tin.

I've explained that it's a tip
But a cosy place
For a coat zip
And don't forget the black shoelace.

Marc Simpson (12)
Fort Hill College, Lisburn

A Poem For Water

The liquid so simple but yet so inviting,
Ripples so gently, but is oh so enticing
We're so lucky water is all around us.
Trickling down the windowpane
It can be refreshing and sweet
As it tickles beneath my feet.
Crashing and dancing boldly against the rocks
Our people have this we are waiting for such
A small thing, but for us so big.
Do we ever *stop* and think about those people?
I hope we do.
Then some day it will be so enticing for them too.

Shannon Bagnall (11)
Fort Hill College, Lisburn

A Hot Summer's Day

It was a hot summer's day,
Where everyone was out to play.
They were laughing and having fun,
In the hot summer's sun.

They were skating and playing football,
Until they burst their ball.
We all had to drink a lot,
Because it was so very hot.

The sun got hotter as the day went on,
Me and my friends we thought we couldn't go on.
We started a water fight
And the boys were full of might.

Soon the day had ended so soon
And people had emptied the paddling pools.
Me and my friends returned to our house
And outside was quiet as a mouse.

Phil McKibben (12)
Fort Hill College, Lisburn

Water

The pitter-pattering of the rain,
Is crashing down the water drain,
The dirty, damp smell,
The rain has lots to tell.

In Malawi the water is too dirty to drink,
I wonder how they manage - just think,
They would like to see the water running down
Through the mountains and streams,
Come on and help them work in teams.

Nicola Hunt (11)
Fort Hill College, Lisburn

Susan

Susan is my bestest pal
We both write with our left hand
We've even got a friend called Sal
Who likes to play in the sand.

She has a rabbit
I have a dog
But we both have a really good habit
Which is sitting on logs.

We've been to the same schools
I like playing footie
We both like going to different pools
And wearing our favourite booties.

We'll be friends to the end
No matter what anyone says
We'll never need to lend
No matter how long the days.

Lee-Ann Graham (12)
Fort Hill College, Lisburn

Talia

Talia your skin is so soft
Like cotton wool
You are as fragile as crystal
You are only brand new
And I love you.
Your fingers are like twigs of a tree
You are like a lamb
You smell like baby powder.

Terry Mairs (13)
Fort Hill College, Lisburn

9/11

On that day I was in school,
I didn't have a clue,
Until I got home,
I wanted to find out.

There were news flashes everywhere,
I found out what happened,
Two planes went into the Twin Towers,
Flames of smoke everywhere.

Firemen running about everywhere,
Trying to save people's lives
This was not an accident,
People thought it was.

People running about screaming,
Some people jumped out of the tower,
They didn't have a choice,
Why did this happen? they ask themselves.

Susan McKnight (13)
Fort Hill College, Lisburn

Football

F ort Hill College I play for
O f course England are the best World Cup team
O wen plays for Liverpool.
T he champs of all time are Real Madrid.
B eckham is the best free-kick taker in the world.
A fter Zidane and Roberto Carlos
L iverpool I love
L eeds I hate.

Alex Gibson (11)
Fort Hill College, Lisburn

Hallowe'en

Something is out there
in the night.
Rustling in the bushes
out of sight.

Looking out the window
what can I see?
Oh there it is
ahh! How can it be?

It's in my garden
it's at the door.
The doorbell rings
my stomach feels poor.

I open the door and . . .
'Trick or treat!'
So you are the ones
roaming the street.

They are children
waiting for me to share.
Oh I'm so silly
they give me a scare.

Terri Houston (12)
Fort Hill College, Lisburn

Matthew

M atthew is my name
A ll my mates call me Briggsy
T hey all like football like me
T hey are in different football teams
H olidays are the best time of the year
E aster is my favourite because of Easter eggs
W hen there is a football pitch free we play football on it.

Matthew Briggs (11)
Fort Hill College, Lisburn

I Am . . .

I am an artist drawing and painting pictures, selling them
and getting them put in museums and other places.

I am a famous actress with long, blonde hair.
I have got lots of money and always wear diamond
jewellery and am starring in the next Hollywood film.

I am a famous pop star, doing concerts all over the UK.
I've got two trophies from the MTV awards.
I've got lots of money and I love my life.

I am a parent looking after my children, bringing them to
school every morning, feeding them and caring for them.

I am the manager of the Odyssey, getting to go backstage
at concerts and getting to meet pop stars like Westlife
and Liberty X.

I am a school teacher listening to people's excuses of how
they have forgotten their homework.

I am Kathy Moore, class 8A1, quite good at maths,
sitting in English, daydreaming through the whole lesson.

Kathy Moore (11)
Fort Hill College, Lisburn

Malawi

A mouth-watering substance dripping from the tap.
A cool and delicious chlorine trap.
Peaceful and calm, explosive and loud.
To play with our family and friends.
Screaming and laughing, the fun never ends.

But in Malawi people cry,
Dirty warm water,
That's all they've got.

Rachael McCready (12)
Fort Hill College, Lisburn

I Am . . .

I am Britney Spears standing backstage in Belfast Odyssey ready to go out and sing in front of millions.

I am in a limo driving through Manchester city with Blue and Westlife sitting at either side of me.

I am in America with all my mates on a full day's shopping spree with £1,000 in my purse.

I am running in the athletics, I have run 25 miles and I have one more mile to go, then all of a sudden I run through the finish line. *I've won the game.*

I am on 'Who Wants To Be A Millionaire' I'm on the last question. Not quite sure but I've picked C, then Chris tells me I have won £1million.

I am Nicole Edmonds, Room 7, listening to our English teacher nagging on at us.

Nicole Edmonds (11)
Fort Hill College, Lisburn

Water Problem

Smelling like chlorine, tasting of salt
Splashing and swimming, such fun
Water fights in the summer sun.
Water, you can have it just turn on the tap
Refreshing, so sweet and cool
We can shape water in ice cube moulds
But Malawi people suffer while we waste
Letting a hose run while washing the car
We always have water to waste on a shower
In Malawi the people are forced to drink
Dirty water filled with germs
Water we take for granted.
So the next time you go to turn on the tap
Stop and think of Malawi.

Melissa Thompson (11)
Fort Hill College, Lisburn

I Am . . .

I am Kelly Osbourne
Loud and tantrum throwing.
Daughter of Mr Rock
Bat-eating Ozzy.

I am Cameron Diaz
The Charlie's Angels babe
Justin Timberlake's girlfriend
How much better could life be?

I am Cat Deeley, live on SMTV
Interviewing pop bands
While fans scream and shout.

I am lying on a beach with Orlando Bloom
The sun beaming down
And waves lapping at our feet.

I am at a rockfest
With my best friends and sister.
Backstage passes in my pocket
Have to go, Sum 41 are waiting.

I am skiing in France
With Avril Lavinge
Flying down the snow hills
And whizzing round corners
Then hit the lodge and bring on the hot chocolate.

I am Samantha Coyle, class 8A1
Room 7, with my nagging English teacher.

Samantha Coyle (12)
Fort Hill College, Lisburn

Fire

F ire is red and fire is hot
I t will burn you as quick as a flash
R oaring red flames here and there
E ven though it is good fun, *take care.*

Nathan Donald (11)
Fort Hill College, Lisburn

Weather

The weather is a mysterious thing
You never know what it will bring.
Some days are wet, some days are dry
It all depends on the look of the sky.

I get confused with all the seasons
As the weather changes for all sorts of reasons.
Summer can be cool, autumn can be not
Winter is not.

Nathan Loughead (12)
Fort Hill College, Lisburn

Catherine

C atherine is what everyone calls me
A nd that's the name I like to be called
T hree honour marks is what I have
H ope I don't get any order marks!
E very day I think about what I'd like to do
R iding horses is my fame
I hope I get some some day
N ow though I just play the piano, lots of songs I play
E ven when I feel unhappy, piano's my thing to do.

Catherine Mercer (11)
Fort Hill College, Lisburn

Water

W ater is all around us
A ll life and Earth need it
T hey cannot live without it
E verywhere we look we see some, like oceans, seas and rivers
R unning down the mountains into our homes and cities.

Daryl Connery (11)
Fort Hill College, Lisburn

I Am . . .

I am a designer, the best in the business,
designing, designing, designing, that's what I do.

I am a pop star, driving through the countryside
in my flash car, singing and dancing on stage.

I am a dolphin trainer, training the dolphins and
whales to obey in a mannerly way.

I am a doctor, helping people get better and
giving people medicine and tablets when they need them.

I am an actress, dressing up, acting in pantomimes
on TV all the time, on EastEnders, Coronation Street
or Emmerdale.

I am a psychiatrist, helping people get over their fears
and coping with life and the way they are.

I am Caaron Garrett, Room 15, good at English,
alright at maths, have to concentrate on my work
to pass my big exam.

Caaron Garrett (11)
Fort Hill College, Lisburn

I Am

I am walking towards the changing rooms with
loads of clothes.

I am getting my make-up and clothes ready for the
big night.

I am getting new shoes to go with the clothes and
make-up.

I am getting ready, it's the big night, I am going to
be a model.

I am Trudi McCourt, only sitting in Mrs Addison's class
daydreaming.

Trudi McCourt (11)
Fort Hill College, Lisburn

Flowers

Flowers, flowers everywhere,
Big ones, small ones, don't pick them.
All they need is sun, water and air.
The water they drink goes up the stem.

Red ones, pink, white and blue,
All different colours and smells.
Don't sniff 'em if you've got the flu,
Or you'll go, *atchoo!*

Summer is the best time of year,
When all the flowers grow and grow,
But don't forget hot weather's here,
For all the flowers to grow and grow.

Autumn's here and flowers die,
We dig them up and throw them away.
Don't cry, do you know why?
Because spring is coming
And you can plant them and play!

Tiffany McAllister (12)
Fort Hill College, Lisburn

I Am . . .

I am Tony Hawks, the best skater in the world, winning the championship 2003.

I am Ray Mysterio, winning the World Heavyweight Championship against Triple H.

I am a member of Black-Eyed Peas, winning the Brit Awards 2004.

I am James Beattie, scoring the winning goal in the World Cup Final 2006.

I am Jordon Foster, Class 8B2, waiting for the home time bell to go.

Jordon Foster (11)
Fort Hill College, Lisburn

Seasons

In the spring when seasons change
When the buds begin to grow
All the lambs in the range
Flowers row on row.

The next season is summer
When we have some fun
The sun gets warmer and warmer
But the fun has just begun.

After that it's autumn
When the leaves begin to fall
It's always so much fun
That's why it's my favourite of all.

Finally it's winter
When the snow will fall
All the lakes freeze over
It's so cold to us all.

Christopher Hull (12)
Fort Hill College, Lisburn

I Am . . .

I am David Blaine, taking big chances, frozen in ice and a water freak.

I am a sailor, good on the seas, but awful at printing and bad like me.

I am Beckham, bender of the ball, top left-hand corner and goals I must score.

I am a golfer, swinging hard at the ball, putting them like Tiger Woods straight on them all.

I am Philip Kinghan in Room 7, staring around me, looking at my mates.

Philip Kinghan (11)
Fort Hill College, Lisburn

Water

We waste it more every day,
We are wasting it without knowing
And the Third World for water they pray
And their crops without water not growing.

We turn on the tap and it always comes,
We use it so often and wastefully,
No water for so long they soon turn numb,
They would be outraged if they could see.

We get cool and clean water from the tap,
We gulp it down as if it grows on trees,
While children cry for it on their parents' laps,
But with no water they don't even have leaves.

We can always take a nice healthy cup,
We are lucky for the unpolluted water we get,
While there's nothing they can do about their lips drying up
And some day I hope we'll help the unfortunate.

Diane Carlisle (13)
Fort Hill College, Lisburn

I Am . . .

I am Tim Howard, keeper for Man United, saving goals left, right and centre or jumping high in the sky.

I am a spaceman in outer space, looking down on the Earth, seeing no people, only water and land. I'm on my way to the moon.

I am an action star, shooting my way through crime.
I am James Bond, known as 007. No one stands in my way.

I am a pop star, getting out of my limo, walking up the red mat onto the stage.

I am Scott Jacques, Class 8B2. Can't wait to get out of English and go home.

Scott Jacques (12)
Fort Hill College, Lisburn

Animals, Animals, Animals

Cute and cuddly
Big and small,
Hairy and furry
I love them all.

Some are small
Some have scales,
Some are tall
Or as big as a whale.

Some eat grass
And some eat meat,
Some eat from my hand
And little fish nibble my feet.

Horses and ponies
Dogs and cats,
They're all so nice
Except for bats.

Ashlea Thompson (12)
Fort Hill College, Lisburn

I Am . . .

I am a superhero flying across towns, saving lives and saving houses. Everyone loves me!

I am a plane flying in the sky, going to Spain, France or even Disneyland. Oh what fun I have.

I am a pop star singing on stage. My tunes are all the rage.

I am a model walking along the catwalk, wearing expensive clothes so everyone can look and admire me.

I am Emma from 8B2. I am in English, daydreaming again.

Emma Ferguson (11)
Fort Hill College, Lisburn

Friends

Friends are brill,
Friends are fun,
Friends bring thrills,
They are little huns!

Friends are cool,
Friends are nuts,
Friends make you drool,
About boys with nice butts!

Friends are sweet,
Friends are sentimental,
Friends give treats,
They are so mental!

Friends are kind,
Friends are caring,
Friends don't mind,
They do everything daring!

Megan Archer (12)
Fort Hill College, Lisburn

Acrostic Poem

K iera is my first name
I was born in January
E nglish is my favourite subject
R achel is my best friend
A fter school I go home and do my homework

R unning is one of my favourite sports
E very Wednesday night I go to GB
I have a cat called Jacko and a dog called Prince
D iving is what I do at the pool.

Kiera Reid (11)
Fort Hill College, Lisburn

Malawi

Water is something we take for granted,
We use it every day in many different ways,
To brush our teeth, to drink, to wash away our pain,
Water that could have been used for something,
Other than flowing down my bathroom drain.

The powerful sound of water,
As it crashes against the rocks,
I sit on a beach and watch
As the waves break against the big boulders of stone
And watch the ripples as the tide goes back out again.

If only I could collect that water
And send it off to Malawi,
Then they would have some pure water,
Not dirty, stale or unpure.
(They don't take water for granted in Malawi).

Jenna Hannigan (12)
Fort Hill College, Lisburn

I Am . . .

I am the champion wrestler, who has defeated everyone who has challenged me.

I am a pop star, singing in front of thousands upon thousands of fans.

I am trapped on a tropical island miles away from shore with servants bringing me anything I want.

I am the first human to go into space, floating about in darkness, looking for undiscovered planets.

I am a magician, performing the greatest magic trick known to man, which is called the Death Saw.

I am Dean Rainey, Class 8A1, good at maths, fair at English and wishing I was at home playing my PlayStation 2.

Dean Rainey (11)
Fort Hill College, Lisburn

I Am . . .

I am on the TV programme Raven, competing for a place
in the final, struggling to complete the tasks.

I am the newest pop star, releasing my new single and
going straight to the number one spot!

I am Angelina Jolie, in for an award at the Oscars,
competing for the title of best actress.
The man says, 'And the nominations for the best actress
are . . . Kate Winslet, Jessie Wallace, Catherine Zeta Jones
and Angelina Jolie . . . the winner is Lara Croft - Angelina Jolie.'

I am Monty's Pass in the Grand National. 1, 2, 3 and over
the fence, galloping on over the next fence. This is the
last fence, galloping on to win. The sweat is lashing off me
at this stage. This is it, the moment has come. *I Win.*

I am on the TV programme 'Who Wants To Be A Millionaire?'
and at the moment I am on the one million pound question.
I answer A and Chris says: 'You have just won one million
pounds! Congratulations!'

I am Kelly Stewart, Class 8A1, sitting in history, bored stiff,
wishing I was at home relaxing.

Kelly Stewart (11)
Fort Hill College, Lisburn

Lovely Water

When the rain falls down,
I always look around,
When I look down at the dirty water,
I see the reflection of my face.

When I drink the lovely fresh water,
I think of people who have none,
So every time I take a drink,
I am glad I have it.

Alana McGahey (12)
Fort Hill College, Lisburn

Pets

I have two cats called Tiger and Pebbles
Pebbles is quite fat
Tiger and Pebbles act like rebels
Tiger will always lie on a mat

They always guard the house
They wait for us to come back
I always see the odd dead mouse
Sometimes even a stack

One time I looked and Pebbles was gone
We all looked everywhere
Tiger knew there was something wrong
We couldn't even find a hair

We found Pebbles in the attic
She had sneaked in
When she got out she stole a haddock
She was so hungry she even ate the fin.

Karl McCready (13)
Fort Hill College, Lisburn

Water

In my house there is a sink,
But do we ever stop to think,
About how clean our tap water is,
As we dilute our orange juice
With its bubbles and fizz?
In Malawi the people suffer in pain,
While we all swim in money and fame.
I never thought of this before
And I would love to open the door
To precious freedom for the country of Malawi.

Sophie Williamson (12)
Fort Hill College, Lisburn

Water

'Where do you get your water from?'

'I turn on a tap in the house and it's there!
I say let's have a water fight
Or fill the pool till it's overflowing
There is plenty of water!
Where do you get your water from?'

'We go to the river and bathe
And we wash our clothes there too.
Our drinking water comes from that same river,
Even though it's dirty and contaminated.'

'Here we pray for sun because it is
Nearly always raining.
Lord please bring the sun.'

'Here we pray for rain to survive,
Please Lord, please may it come.'

Victoria Stuart (12)
Fort Hill College, Lisburn

Brian

My horse is called Brian,
He is dark brown,
Like the colour of a hazelnut.
He loves to eat grass,
My dad calls him a lawnmower.
I go for gallops across the fields,
With the wind blowing through his mane.
When we get back I let him back into his field,
He loves to go for a roll, flattening dough.
I love my horse, Brian.

Leanne Nelson (13)
Fort Hill College, Lisburn

Water

As I entered the swimming pool
all I could smell was the sweet chlorine.
I ducked my head under the water
and counted to ten.

I went down the slides
and started splashing the dripping water
all over my friend.
I was having such fun
I hoped the pleasure would never end.

As I stood in the changing room
water dripped from my hair,
Then I told my friend to say ya dare.

At the end
I drove my father round the bend.

Zara Diamond (11)
Fort Hill College, Lisburn

I Am . . .

I am a policeman with the navy-blue and white uniform,
driving a blue, yellow and white car, going to a riot.

I am a football player who is playing for Manchester United,
going out onto the pitch in my red shirt and white shorts,
going to have a match against Arsenal.

I am a very wealthy man who has a big mansion out in the
countryside with sports cars and butlers.
I can buy anything in sight.

I am a famous wrestler winning all my fights and giving out
autographs and getting good money.
My brother would be dead jealous.

I am Nathan Stephens, Class 8B1.
Bad at maths, good at science and fair at art and design.
I need to improve on my maths.

Nathan Stephens (12)
Fort Hill College, Lisburn

I Am . . .

I am a rock star; our band is called 'Contained 56'.
I am the guitarist for it. Jumping around with sweat
pouring down my face.

I am a movie star, practising my lines all the time,
focusing on every word. The movie director always
shows me a thumbs up.

I am the richest person in the world. I have a castle as my home,
a widescreen TV and servants, a swimming pool in my bathroom
and a Jacuzzi too.

I am a computer freak. I fix computers and have the best games,
I beat everyone at them!

I am in the army, shooting all the targets and being careful
when using the 'rocket launchers'.

I am the world's greatest author, so far I have written 67 books,
and all my stories are very long.

I am in the final, I am against Tony Hawks in a skateboarding match,
the crowd go wild! An hour late of excitement, I win!

I am Becky Lee, class 8A1, good at history, poor at English,
like reading in English though! But Mrs Addison is talking and
I'm not listening . . . wait a minute . . . she's just asked me a question!

Becky Lee (11)
Fort Hill College, Lisburn

Water

W ater is what you need to keep you alive in
A frica, they don't have a lot of water
T o drink from and grow crops with
E verybody needs water to live and
R ain is rare in a lot of countries.

Jasmine Gillett (11)
Fort Hill College, Lisburn

Homework

Homework marks are out of 91,
An honour mark is for me,
When I have three,
So I always must be smart and good
And do my homework as I should.
If I don't hand it in on time,
An order mark will be mine.

Kirsty Scott (11)
Fort Hill College, Lisburn

Water

W ater is everywhere in Northern Ireland, we take it for granted.
A frica doesn't have very much water, they have
T o drink very dirty water,
E very woman has to go and collect water from miles away.
R ivers are where we get our water and deep down in the ground too.

Rachel Hayes (11)
Fort Hill College, Lisburn

My Water Poem

Water is vital for life
And if it's clean it is better
Some people have to drink dirty water
And they can die from it
Even water you think is clean can have germs in it
If there are rocks in a river they will purify the water.

Andrew Agnew (11)
Fort Hill College, Lisburn

Malawi

Where is the rain I'd like to know
So maybe some day our crops could grow.

While people have water fights far away, at home
And others have bubble baths full of foam,
Children are crying from hunger and pain
Hoping someday God will bring rain

People waste water without care
Not thinking of them being in despair.
Our land is dry, barren and crisp,
And we can't farm in our large forests.

People hate the rain in faraway lands
While we would love to feel it pitter-patter on our hands.
All we want is some food and water
And for our country to be less hotter!

Some want the opposite of this
And I know that it would be missed.

Lyndsey Smyth (12)
Fort Hill College, Lisburn

A Poem About Me

D avid's my name but I used to
A lways be called Davy.
V ery hard working, I think
I also try to be neat and helpful and
D o my best in everything.

G regg is my surname
R unning is my hobby
E than is my best friend
G eography is one of my favourite subjects
G lad in everything I do!

David Gregg (11)
Fort Hill College, Lisburn

Malawi

Why does the rain not fall?
Crops drying up in the sun
No clean water anywhere
What have we done to deserve this?

Around the world water falls,
Like a light waterfall.
Water from a tap,
In a swimming pool,
From a shower at night.

Water is slippery, wet, thirst-quenching
Screaming water fights; water laying everywhere,
Water running down a stream,
Crashing on rocks.

As the people of Malawi pray and cry,
'What have we done to deserve this?'

Sheryl White (12)
Fort Hill College, Lisburn

I Am . . .

I am a famous pop star doing a dance routine on stage,
the crowds are clapping and cheering, going wild.

I am the world champion swimmer,
speeding through the cold, clear water.

I am shopping in Hollywood,
spending lots of money.

I am meeting Westlife
and I am becoming their friend.

I am lying in my warm bed, drinking hot chocolate
on a winter's morning.

I am Sarah Maxwell, class 8A1,
good at English, not so good at maths.

Sarah Maxwell (11)
Fort Hill College, Lisburn

I Am

I am a fighter pilot, zooming through the air,
returning to base, preparing again.

I am a movie star, getting out of my Ferrari,
waving at the crowd, posing for the press.

I am the commander of a naval battleship,
shooting into enemy cities, supporting the ground troops.

I am Michael Owen, pro football player,
running onto the pitch at Anfield, waving to my fans.

I am a millionaire, walking out of my mansion,
having a hard life choosing to drive my Ferrari, Lotus, Jaguar or TVR.

I am a skydiver, zooming towards the earth,
the wind blowing in my face, opening my chute, floating to earth.

I am Ethan Megrath, class 8A1, dreadful at maths,
fair at everything else, must concentrate.

Ethan Megrath (12)
Fort Hill College, Lisburn

Myself

N eil is my name and I like sports.
E very day I go outside and play football or other activities.
I also enjoy playing rugby and going swimming. I
L ove listening to music, going to the cinema and going up to the
   town with my mates.

I n the summer of 2003 I went to Ibiza and it was a
R are opportunity to see the sunset and the sea. It
W as a great holiday and I hope some year
I will go back. It was fun and I did
N ot want to go home. I was sad when I had to leave.

Neil Irwin (11)
Fort Hill College, Lisburn

I Am . . .

I am walking onto the pitch at Old Trafford
with the rest of the team and the other mascots as the fans roar.

I am walking into Ibrox Stadium to watch an old firm derby
between Rangers and Celtic as all the fans sing.

I am in Spain training with David Beckham
and after that going around the town.

I am playing in the World Cup final for Northern Ireland
against USA and I have just scored the winning goal.

I am a millionaire stepping out of my blue BMW convertible
at the premiere of my new movie.

I am on a beach in the Bahamas with the sun
beaming down on me and a nice cold drink in my hand.

I am Aimée Harbinson, sitting in English,
wishing the last hour would fly by.

Aimée Harbinson (12)
Fort Hill College, Lisburn

I Am . . .

I am the inline skater for Great Britain, going into the finals of the X Games, the crowd go wild as I make a 900° grab over the 2 metre gap!

I am the runner in the final of the Olympic games.
Getting closer to the finish line, I pass the finish line and win!

I am a cartoon artist designing a cartoon, then the cartoon
comes to life and it is amazing then it stops and gives me an idea.

I am Triple X doing a wild and extreme, also insane, stunt, I take a car, go onto a ship, then drive off the ship into the sea.

I am in the newest rock band, the 'Electric Eels'. I play base and we hit number one with the song we wrote called 'Skate Don't Walk'.

I am Conor McCahon from 8A1, good at science, OK at English,
and bad at history, but still trying my best . . .

Conor McCahon (11)
Fort Hill College, Lisburn

My Acrostic Poem

A ndrew is what my parents call me
N athan is the name of my best friend
D rawing is what I like doing as well as
R ollerblading up and down my street
E ating is what I like to do
W hales are my favourite animals.

Andrew Maye (11)
Fort Hill College, Lisburn

When I Grow Up!

When I grow up what will I be?
Is there a future in store for me?
Will I be a chauffeur and drive a big car,
Or be a supermodel or a TV star?
I could be the world's greatest cook,
Become an author and write a book,
I could be a housewife and stay at home all day,
Better be a rock star to get more pay.
I could be a policewoman and help fight crime,
Maybe go on stage at a pantomime.
Or I could be a lawyer and sort out ordeals,
Or own a restaurant and create great meals.
I could be a brilliant teacher, the favourite at school,
I could be a doctor or nurse, that would be cool.
I could own a hotel, oh what a dream,
Or even join a racing team.
I could travel the world in eighty days,
Swim with dolphins in Miami bays.
Some day I could be Queen,
But for now I am happy as a teen.
I may even become a vet,
I don't know just yet.
I have all the time I need to see,
In the future what I'll be!

Kerry-Ann McMackin (13)
Loreto Grammar School, Omagh

Get Well Soon

I hope that I get well sooner, not later,
For I dearly miss my hot water bottle,
Not to mention the food at home,
If I get back there, I'll never moan,
Here it's cold tea and toast,
It's no wonder the cook can't boast,
Of his watery scrambled eggs and lumpy custard,
Dinner with no sauce, salt or mustard.
Here it's starchy clothes and sheets,
A broken telly and lumpy seats,
Patients coughing, groaning, snoring,
No books or visitors, it's so boring!
When I leave here I'll complain no more,
'Goodbye!' I'll say as I go out the door.

Grainne McGread (13)
Loreto Grammar School, Omagh

My Passion

My mum says I eat them for
Breakfast, dinner and tea
And that it is impossible to get work out of me.
Jacqueline Wilson, Roald Dahl,
J K Rowling, Diane Hoh.
Get my drift, now you know
What I'm talking about,
Books of course!

They're my passion, my fashion
They're what make me tick
When my head is in a book
You won't get a second look.

Some people rap, some rock and roll
Some people bungee, some people bowl
But give me a book and you've got me *hooked!*

Lauren Harper (11)
Loreto Grammar School, Omagh

The Future

When we look into the future
Who knows where we'll be.
So many opportunities out there
Just waiting for you and me.

Some people think of school days
And say they're the best.
However they're hard to get through
They just seem like one big test.

How many times can we say
That we've wanted to be older?
But when some people get there
They just want to cry on a shoulder.

Who knows what the future will bring
What's meant to be will be.
The annoying thing is
We have to wait and see.

Verity Mayers (14)
Loreto Grammar School, Omagh

In Dreams

I dreamed of you last night, Grandad,
I dreamed you were at my side.
I saw you reading your paper,
But you weren't there, my heart lied.

I dreamed of you last night,
I dreamed I told you of my day.
I heard you laugh at all my jokes,
'Young you know, no sense you see,'
Is what I heard you say.

I dreamed of you last night,
Before I could speak, you slipped away.
Only in dreams now, can I tell you this,
I'll love and remember you, come what may.

Fionnuala Hinds (15)
Loreto Grammar School, Omagh

A Day In The Life Of A Teen

Get up in the morning and fix my hair,
Go out without make-up, would you dare?
On goes the eye shadow, lipgloss and all,
Where shall I go, the town, the mall?

Into 'Tammy' with its shoes and clothes galore,
Baggy trousers and tops, it's one of thee stores.
Then into 'Claire's' with its bobbles and bags
Chains and rings with all their own tags.

When back at home I'll listen to pop,
When a good song comes on I don't want it to stop.
I'll sit back in my chair and sing along,
Most of the time I get the words wrong!

Sit up in bed and play with my phone,
Writing by text, I've finally got my own!
Playing 'snake' and listening to it bleep
Then lie down for some beauty sleep.

Charlene McCarron (14)
Loreto Grammar School, Omagh

Winter

Snow is falling to the ground,
Soft white blanket on the ground.

Children playing, have snowball fights,
Most people find it such a delight.

Christmas trees shining bright,
It gets dark before it's night.

Children writing letters to the big man himself,
And we must not forget those helpful elves.

We all love Christmas, it is a great season,
But we must not forget that special reason!

Rebecca Andrews (12)
Methodist College, Belfast

Time . . .

One part is over,
One path is ended,
When something ends,
They say something begins.

Another path begins to grow,
What will it bring,
And how will I cope?
Time will tell.
Time will show.

Will this fresh path bring you?
Whoever you may be.
Who will it take?
Who will it bring?
Time will tell.
Time will show.

Hopes, dreams and future lie ahead.
Ugly, bad or wonderful?
Nobody to take my hand and show me.
Only people to guide and help me.
Who knows . . .?
Time will tell,
And time will show.

Amy Stubbings (16)
Methodist College, Belfast

Shadow Of Death

Youth is lost in the shadow.
Boys become men,
Men become boys.
Those who pass through,
Are scarred beyond time.

Mark Elliott (15)
Methodist College, Belfast

I Am In Love

Roses are red
Violets are blue
I am in love
I hope you are too
I wish I could see
See you here with me

When we first met
The sun started to set
But now that I've grown
I'm starting to moan
I don't like you anymore
Because of your noisy snore

I hate you now
You look more like a cow
You smell like a rat
That's just sat in a cow pat
All I am saying is I'm dumping you
And that you smell like something from the zoo.

Philip Smyth (12)
Methodist College, Belfast

A Special Winter's Night

Tonight is the night that kids dream of
A big red man coming from above.
He has a white beard and white hair too.
Giving presents to anyone who's been good
But if you've been bad you won't get presents -
You'll get a pot of coal,
And once that night's over,
Mum and Dad, I hope you're sober
Because you've got Christmas dinner to make!

Niall Annett (12)
Methodist College, Belfast

Can I Keep The Suit And Boots?

'Can I keep the suit and boots, Sir?'
I heard the young lad say
'Sure, Son, just sign here
And you'll soon be on your way!'

His better life was soon undone
Deep in a stinking trench
Feet rotting, suit torn
Rats and lice crawling in the stench

Screaming shells and exploding bombs
A nightmare world with no true dawn
The threat of death all around
This young lad, a helpless pawn

'Over the top,' the order came
The lad surged forward, for his country's gain
The hail of bullets thudded deep,
Another young life snatched in vain.

Robert Coburn (16)
Methodist College, Belfast

The Night's Not Over Yet

As I peer down the street,
The only thing I see is,
The children all out playing trick or treat,
All their bags are full of sweets,
But still they call door to door collecting more treats,
The fancy dress, the brooms and funny masks,
How I wish I were young again so I could do all these funny tasks,
A pumpkin's burning low as the night begins to end,
The night's not over yet as some creatures set their trend,
They come out from bins and cracks among the street,
Mostly strange children looking to collect strange treats,
They look around the shops but everyone's asleep,
They should have come out earlier and caught the last,
                              of the midnight treats.

Lisa McKim (13)
Methodist College, Belfast

Fear Of Doubting

Why do we live
Or do we just exist?
Why do we love
Or is it even real?
I held my lover in my arms
And lived a life of fear.
Fear for losing one so loved
Fear for nothing in return.
Why do I love?
I do not know.
Why do I care?
Please let me know.

A truth is in a lie
A lie is in a truth.
A laugh is in a sob
A tear comes with a smile.
But when I am with you
I do not lie
For fear of doubting truth.

I look for you in a crowded room
Until you shine a light
One laugh
One look
One smile I see
A prod
A touch
A quiet word.

Oh let me see
Oh let me be
With you
In light:
Never will I flee.

Debi Moore (17)
Methodist College, Belfast

Winter

Winter is my favourite season.
I bet you want to know the reason,
I was born in a hurry on a starry night,
Christmas Eve suited me just right.

Winter's full of parties and fun you see,
And not just to celebrate little old me,
Jesus was born in a stable back when,
The star appeared with the three wise men!

I love to build snowballs and wrap up snug,
And build a big snowman and give him a hug,
With his carrot nose and his coal-black eyes,
He's sure to give the neighbours a big surprise.

I love the snowflakes and their taste in my mouth,
And the way all the birds know to fly south,
I love to go sledging, down the big hill,
And even when I topple I get a big thrill.

The bare trees look special clothed in snow,
Their skeleton shapes really seem to glow,
Jack Frost coats everything that he meets
And the glimmer brightens up the streets.

Our Christmas dinner is a real big treat,
With an enormous turkey instead of meat,
Brussels sprouts are not my thing
But the Christmas pudding makes me sing.

So you can see that winter is the best,
Even if you need to wear more than one vest,
With my hat, my gloves and my wellies on,
I'm more than ready for this season.

Anna Coburn (12)
Methodist College, Belfast

One

Pages loosely folded,
As if they are there to be read,
But no one will read them,
No one can see the words
Imprinted on the paper.
They do not matter,
Do not seem special,
Like you.
You aren't special.
You are merely another person,
Another mouth to feed,
Another body to clothe,
Another present to buy,
Another word to write
On the back of a photograph.
But maybe you are special.
They cannot see you,
As they cannot see the words
That mean something.
They cannot see the truth that you are,
Your honesty,
Individuality.

Hannah Wilson (14)
Methodist College, Belfast

Autumn

Leaves falling all around
Twirling and gently
Landing on the ground

Leaves of all colours, crimson
Yellow, brown and gold
Falling off as the weather gets cold

Now the trees have no leaves
They look like wooden skeletons
Swaying in the breeze.

Julia McClure (12)
Methodist College, Belfast

My Family And Me

My dad told me to be quiet
My mum told me to shut up
My brother's music is rocking
And my sister's putting on too much make-up.

The cat's scratching the curtains
The dog is barking outside
I really don't think I'll make it out
Of the house alive.

My gran's crying for a cup of tea
The baby needs a change, he's done a pee
The dinner has fallen on the floor
My cousin is being such a bore.

Well, that's all about my family
I think that's it, well that's what
I want it to be.

Louise Magee (13)
Methodist College, Belfast

Coalition Of The Willing

Foreign policy and private talks will decide
If the path is taken once again
Of death and decay in foreign places
Or of safety and sleep in one's own bed.
As the sun mercilessly bakes the sand
For it cares not for these petty fools,
Troops prepare and await their orders
Civilians gather their family to them in fear
A shadow cast over them by a threat.
Their fate lies with more important men
Men who will not have to fight
To feel disgust at the murdering monsters they have become
Or wake up from a nightmare of the blood on their hands.
Men whose families will not feel the pain of losing a loved one to war.

Ashleigh Craig (15)
Methodist College, Belfast

Portugal

I said to my mum, I wanted to go somewhere sunny,
I wanted to go somewhere hot,
I wanted to go somewhere foreign,
She said, 'Too bad, *you're not!*'

I wanted to sit on sandy beaches,
I wanted a gorgeous tan,
I wanted to swim in the warm seas,
And spot a nice-looking man.

I thought, *what place could I go to?*
What place would have all my list?
Then I thought, *Portugal would be brilliant*
No fog, no cloud and no mist.

I ran and begged my mum,
To see if I could go,
She thought I was being so silly,
And said, *'No! No! No!'*

For the next few weeks I was miserable,
I cried and cried and *cried!*
Until my mum said, 'Alright, we'll go!'
Now I knew I had seen her nice side!

PS I had a great time in Portugal!

Ryan Maxwell (12)
Methodist College, Belfast

My Best Friend

Friends come and go,
Best friends always stay,
We're always fun and hyper,
Our smiles don't go away!

I've seen your teardrops fall,
You're seen me fill up too,
Always by my side,
Always me and you!

Vanessa Cotter (13)
Methodist College, Belfast

My Dream That Never Came True!

All my life I've been searching,
For someone just like you.
I never thought it would be this night
That it actually came true.
You're all I ever hoped for,
You were always in my dreams,
Which is now reality it seems.

Your dark brown eyes and thick black hair,
I can't help but stop and stare.
You really are perfect in every way,
You can be sure I will love you for more than one day.

But then the heavens closed and up opened Hell!
Because all that lay ahead of me was a cheap liar,
And heartbreaker.
For this was no perfect guy,
But an unfaithful boy not worthy of my love
'How could you?' I scream!
All he shouts back is, 'That's life, go back to your dream!'

Hannah Strudley (15)
Methodist College, Belfast

Autumn

In autumn the leaves are golden brown,
And yellow and orange and red.
And you wrap up in lots of clothes
From your toes up to your head.
Outside is frosty,
With ice and snow,
And all the birds get up and go,
Apart from the robin, who stays at home
And who doesn't mind the snow or ice
And when all the other birds leave for the south
He stays at home, cosy and nice.

Clare Mackey (12)
Methodist College, Belfast

Thinking Of Christmas

On a cold winter's morning
The snow lying softly on the ground
The sound of children playing
Makes you think of Christmas.

On a cold winter's afternoon
The smell of a hot lunch in a house
The sound of talk and a laugh
Makes you think of Christmas.

On a cold winter's evening,
The light sound of the children breathing in bed
The sight of trees and decorations up
Makes you think of Christmas.

On a cold winter's night
The silence of the house and gently falling snow
The sound of the creaking floorboards
Makes you think of Christmas.

Aron Hamilton (12)
Methodist College, Belfast

Mad About Rugby

They're gathering in Australia,
For a grand old rugby show,
20 teams from around the world
Down under they will go.

The greats of rugby will be there,
To claim the greatest prize.
Springbok, Celt and wallaby,
And men of every size.

My dad is going, lucky bloke
Adelaide and Sydney too.
The men in green he will support
And see the whole thing through

Luke Acheson (13)
Methodist College, Belfast

Death And Death

'All our dreams will at last come alive'
Soldiers sang to themselves that morn
They tied up their laces with smiles on their faces
Thinking they'd win at the Somme
But how wrong they would be, how terribly wrong
As they marched to the Somme early that dawn

The air seemed still as the men marched along
The stars still visible in the dusty skies
Their minds were weary, their feet felt heavy
Yet hope shone bright in their bloodshot eyes
If only they had known before they commenced
That the battle would end in sad consequence

The ground seemed to give way beneath their feet
Some ran, some staggered, some fell
But all the men in their hearts felt the same
They were trapped between gunfire and Hell
The guns drowned out their silent screams
And shattered all their hopes and dreams.

Karishma Kusurkar (15)
Methodist College, Belfast

Hallowe'en Rap

I saw the Grim Reaper,
He was outside my house,
I ran down the stairs and chased him out,
I chased him round the front,
I chased him round the back,
He fell on the ground,
I hit him on the head until he was dead,
I called the cops,
To pick him up,
When the cops came,
He was gone.

David Martin (12)
Methodist College, Belfast

Paint

Paints of every colour
on my palette they sit,
mix the colours
carefully, you don't know
what you'll find
but you know the
magical colours you've
painted in your mind.

A flick here and a stroke there,
a splash here and a splash there,
Jackson Pollock, here I come.

Van Gogh's yellow paints
a perfect September sun,
Picasso pink plums fall
to the umber grass,
Rothko's burnt orange
dances from the trees,
while Raoul Dufy's
Blue Birds swoop down
to perch on the eaves.

Muted coloured seeds
in Rembrandt hues and
Gauguin's pinky sky meets
where the hills gently lie.

Sophia McKeever (12)
Methodist College, Belfast

The Rats Of War

I can hear them chewing,
Constantly chewing,
Kings at a feast
Of the rotting dead.

I can see them moving,
Maliciously searching,
For another limp finger
Or a chunk of a head.

I can sense them sneering,
Gloating and sneering,
As men come for glory
Have perished instead.

I can smell them always,
Revolting, disgusting,
They smell only weakness,
Know I haven't been fed.

I can feel them near me,
Patiently waiting,
As I lie here dying
In my flea-ridden bed.

I know they are coming,
Feeding and killing,
Soon it is my turn
To be led into Hell.

Ryan Deane (16)
Methodist College, Belfast

Thirst

On and on the war kept going
Some days sunny, others snowing
Soldiers dying all the time
Conscripts replacing them on the front line

Rats in trenches running around
Trying to find food along the ground
Bodies will do, as they're something to eat
But they left the soldiers' rotting feet

Up the line the British advanced
But through this move their lives they chanced
They heard the sounds of the German gun
And feared their lives were almost done

The weary soldiers continued to fight
Through long, long days and hard, dark nights
All they wanted was to see a light
To show them that things would be alright

The men spent days hearing horrid sounds
Within their heads they sounded round and round
No-man's-land was the men's deathbed
'We're sorry they're gone,' was all that was said

The men were ordered out to their death
On the battlefield they took their last breath
All because of man's thirst for power
But one man's thirst went too far!

Colin Kirkpatrick (15)
Methodist College, Belfast

The Burglar

The back door opens with a squeak and then is quietly shut,
Footsteps move silently across the newly washed kitchen floor,
Leaving traces of mud behind.
Into the front room they go, staying there for a while
Then out of the room with a rustle.
Down the hall, come the soft sound of the footsteps
                                        along the floorboards.
Up the stairs goes the sound
The muffled tread two at a time.
Darkness causes hesitation,
One door is opened and the sound enters the room
Shadows bounce off the walls.
The squeaking of drawers can be heard coming from bedrooms.
Tiptoeing up another flight of stairs and down again,
Quietly. Quietly! Quietly!
Flash! Buzz! The lights go on, the alarm goes off.
So bright, so loud!
Bags are dropped.
The sound of running feet.
Down the stairs five at a time.
Jumping! Gasping!
Along the hall. Door flung open.
Out into the street.
Running steps fading away.
Muffled.

Megan Lynn (12)
Methodist College, Belfast

The Order

The moonlight was patchy as it broke through
The low-lying mist on no-man's land.
An eerie silence could be felt by each man still waiting
For that excuse that would save them from the massacre ahead.
It seemed like an eternity at the bottom of those rungs,
Studying the wood grain and every splinter.
I grabbed my rifle, hands white and knuckles blue with cold.
No time was given to thought as the order came through
And we burst over the top, running and screaming.
I felt a pain explode somewhere in my legs
And my body buckled beneath me as a new sort of fatigue
Settled upon me.
My head rested upon the vast muddy field and
I drifted away to a calm . . .
The moonlight was patchy as it broke through the low-lying mist
                                                        on no-man's-land.

Andrew Gerard (15)
Methodist College, Belfast

The Final Charge

Along the trenches silence fell,
Not a man dared even draw breath,
Soon they would charge at the jaws of Hell,
And meet their untimely death.

'Why are we fighting this pointless war?
Why do we go through this suffering and pain?
Who are we fighting and dying for?
What do the generals hope to gain?'

The soldiers fell, one by one
Their bodies torn asunder.
Cut down by shell, gas and gun,
Because of the general's blunder.
All around the battlefield their bodies lay,
Soon forgotten and buried in foreign clay.

Chuan Hong (16)
Methodist College, Belfast

The First Of July

'Twas the first of July, nineteen-sixteen
The buttons on jackets were perfectly clean,
Three Irish divisions ready to go,
How many returned? Nobody quite knows.

For six months on end, the men had been sat
In waterlogged trenches, infested with rats.
Morale had suffered, friends had died
The condemned men's last meal, a good Ulster fry.

The order was given at quarter-past six,
But the Hun had been up to their usual tricks,
When the shelling had started, they fled underground
Yet the Irishmen thought they'd see corpses around.

So over the top, the Irishmen hopped,
The guns did their job, like flies the men dropped.
Still they continued, and made great gains,
But too many died, too many were maimed.

Every year, on the first of July,
Think of those men who said their goodbyes
To parents, brothers, sons and wives
Before at the Somme, they all lost their lives.

Colin Williamson (15)
Methodist College, Belfast

Murderous Maths

I thought maths would be fun
I guess I'm just dumb
I thought I'd be good at it
I guess someone needs to give me a hit
It was my best subject at primary school
But when I answered that question about fractions
I just looked like a fool!
I didn't think maths would be hard
But really, when it comes to it,
I am just a coward!

Gareth Reilly (11)
Methodist College, Belfast

Questions Of Anticipation

Today is it?
The time is now
It shall all unfold from here
The question is just how?

My true friends shall come
When? I wish I had a clue
A fresh clean sheet, friends to make
The question is just who?

Seven years ahead
In which will happen such a lot
If I put in effort I'll get something out
The question is just what?

10am shall come I know
Once again I check for my pen
10 o'clock must come at last
The question is just when?

Nicola Wright (12)
Methodist College, Belfast

Chin Up

Down in the trenches where we all stood,
The shells and the gunfire dictating the mood.
Getting ready to go over - it was the first day of the Somme
'Can't wait 'til it's all finished,' said a weary soldier, Tom.

The General marched up and down the rows, as ever looking glum,
He said, 'Chin up,' to Jimmy, who replied, 'I want my mum.'
The noise had stopped but then we heard the signal whistle blow,
So it was one foot on the ladder, up and over we go.

Rifles pointed forwards, into no-man's land we went
Dodging the German machine guns, some of the lads already spent.
The battlefield was muddy and dark, the grass no longer green,
Then came the shrapnel in the shell, that blasted us to smithereens!

Katherine Ross (15)
Methodist College, Belfast

Reality

Confusing darkness,
Rancid smell all around.
Walls of disease-ridden rats,
And floors of dead, rotting bodies.

Muffled complaining whispers,
Falling shrapnel like evil rain.
Awake all night long
Tot of rum keeps you going.

Eyes filled with pain,
Of friends since childhood.
Incompetent fools for officers,
We could do a better job.

Excitement and glory of war is vanished,
Cold reality has hit us.
The suit and boots aren't worth it
But you can't be a coward
You can't go home.

Hannah Litvack (15)
Methodist College, Belfast

Then And Now

The expanse between us lies twisted and tangled
Swamped in blood, and mud, and debris
The grey air exploding, flashing, filled with smoke

Around me, men die while the filthy rats thrive
Feasting on flesh, dead or alive
Crimson, brown and grey mix together in confusion

Standing now, 30 years on
Nothing disturbs the silence of the Somme
So unearthly quiet and still
Ally and enemy united in death

Still the long, wet, muddy days play in my mind
And will stay there, engraved, to the end of my time.

Rachel Finlay (15)
Methodist College, Belfast

Reality

Behind me the general sits,
In his comfy home.
Playing a game
With toy soldiers and battlefields.
How can it all be real?

In front of me the Germans wait,
Trench upon trench.
Their guns are ready
To cause death and destruction.
How can it all be real?

Around me my friends stand,
All from a single street.
Once ready for action
Now resigned to fate.
How can it all be real?

Below me the rats run,
Fat from the many dead.
Even the mud cannot stop them
Though it bloody well stops us.
How can it all be real?

On me the lice feed,
The scratching never ceases.
In my clothes they live
No better accommodation than raw flesh.
How can it all be real?

Over the top I go,
At last the day has come.
Through the smoke, over the wire,
Towards the machine gun fire.
How can it all be real?

Kirsty McDonald (15)
Methodist College, Belfast

Medals For Murder - Views Of A Pacifist

I wonder why 'war heroes' are so honoured.
The medals pinned on their blazers drip with blood.
We commemorate the killing and the violence
Of the blood feasts.

I sympathise with the soldiers,
Wading knee-deep in mud and corpses
Surrounded with the thick stench of combat.
But they signed up, did they not?

War is a creation of the power-hungry.
The soldiers are brainwashed by society
To think they were dying bravely.
How does one die bravely
When shot in the chest by 'the enemy'?
Fall without a sound,
Or let out last breath with a cry?

The laws of our land say, 'Thou should not murder',
Yet war posters are phrased, 'Fight for your country'.
I can't comprehend the ways of our government,
All their laws that contradict,
That killing is encouraged for warfare
While there are 'criminals' punished
For essentially the same deeds.

Veterans celebrated with parades.
Prisoners paraded to their death
Why should any be idolised
For inflicting pain on others?
There's no such thing
As a just kill!

Sharon Ross (15)
Methodist College, Belfast

Seasons

Summer
The blazing hot sun
The ice cream disappearing
Children are swimming.

Autumn
The trees, bare and cold
The leaves dancing in the wind
Rainbow in the sky

Winter
The snowmen stand cold
The crisp air blows across my face
The land covered in white

Spring
The animals awake
The flowers begin to grow
The land is green again.

Catherine Dugan
Methodist College, Belfast

War!

Husbands, sons, fathers and fiancés
Some just one to others, but the great deal are more
Different stories but all hear the same call
That from their country help her stand tall

We'll be under attack if we don't do something now
So let's make a great army, it's obvious of course
But what's this? They're not backing down!
So let's make an even bigger army; break them down with brute force

They don't think of peace talks
Both sides want more than is fair
Bartering for more than is their own share
But after all the army's still there
Condemned to the bidding of the men who know best.

Karl Irwin (15)
Methodist College, Belfast

A Sweet Tooth

The school bell rings,
It's that time again,
We're off to the sweet shop,
Me and my friends.

We race down the street,
Burst through the door,
The bell above tinkles,
As our feet patter on the floor.

The old lady appears,
Looks at us three,
Gives a little smile,
As we stare around in glee.

Gobstoppers, cola bottles,
Little white mice,
Strawberry bootlaces,
At not a bad price!

We all look around us,
These things are our life!
We better choose wisely,
And get something nice.

We hand out our money,
And receive our sweets,
We say, 'Thank you,'
And go off to eat.

Munch! Crunch
Suck! Fizz!
Pop! Bang!
Our taste buds whiz!

And tomorrow we'll be back
Getting our fill,
We eat so many
And we *never* get ill (touch wood)!

Thomas Olver (11)
Methodist College, Belfast

Voices

A voice will tell me what to write,
It whispers in my ear,
He or she, I cannot tell - though it often does appear.
Its words transfer to paper,
What my own lips cannot tell,
It speaks of Heaven, Limbo and the journey down to Hell.

The voice - it comes too often -
It plagues me in my head,
Tries, tears and tortures 'til my mind it swells and swells.

With stories of other places,
My brain will some day burst,
And that I enjoy the voice,
It makes it even worse.

Devil, muse or goddess,
Or forgotten part of me,
Its eyes, not mine, see things no others see.

And I - its helpless little fool -
Must write 'til my body's done,
And then the voice, consuming voice,
Will move to another poor someone.

Finola Austin (12)
Methodist College, Belfast

Paul Ward, RBHSC

Hollow walls
And baby calls.

A faceless doctor's case
On a diagnostic race

Battle sign
No decline.

Endless hours
Waiting for paracetamol's powers.

I fell out of bed
And banged my head.

Couldn't hear out of an ear
And the NHS paid dear.

Thought I had an ear infection
That was medical neglection.

The hospital food left something to be desired
Luckily, I was very tired.

I'm off games 'til November
This event I'll always remember.

Michael Boyle (12)
Methodist College, Belfast

I Spend My Day

I spend my day
Doing things my way
Watching humans sleep
Munching while I eat

I spend my day
Keeping boredom at bay
Playing chasies round the garden
Saying 'Please' and 'Pardon?'

I spend my day
Enjoying the month of May
Sniffing the bunches of flowers
Left on the step by Mrs Powers

I spend my day
Snuggling up in the hay
Twitching out of habit
And if you haven't guessed . . . I'm a rabbit!

Maeve Middleton (12)
Methodist College, Belfast

My Dog Tess

She is a lovely puppy dog.
She bounces around like a frog!
She has lovely curly, wavy hair.
It's golden brown, no, more like fair.
She has a beautiful, straight, waggy tail,
After an accident, her back leg's frail.

She creeps upstairs late at night
And sometimes causes quite a fright,
When we find she's gone and fled
We find her curled up on the end of the bed!
I really love my puppy, Tess,
She totally is the very *best!*

Holly Collins (11)
Methodist College, Belfast

My Dog

I have a small dog, who is the colour of soot,
You have to be very careful not to kick him with your foot!
The problem is he is so small and very dark, besides
He would be no good for giving little children rides.

But my wee dog is so special to me, he knows how to make a fuss,
Because of the way he plays with me and next-door's cat called Gus.
He always gives you a welcome which cheers me when I am blue
He always wants me to play ball even when I tell him I'm through.

When he has a Jumbone, be careful, don't go near him
Else you may find that you could lose a limb.
One day he went through the window onto the roof
We said, 'Oscar, come back.' He said, 'Woof woof!'

My little dog, Oscar, is a great wee friend,
Even though sometimes he drives me round the bend.
I wouldn't be without him, he is a lovely wee guy,
He is nearly as good as my mum's special apple pie.

Christian Douglas (12)
Methodist College, Belfast

Judge

The seas were wild,
But skies were tame,
The horse was fit,
But its spirit was lame,

The body was strong,
But the soul was weak,
The ears listened,
But the mouth would never speak,

His form was confident,
But his mind was unsure,
Outside she was dirty,
Inside she was pure.

Aimee Muirhead (12)
Methodist College, Belfast

The Dancer!

If you were to glance at her,
You'd *know* she was a dancer.

As graceful as a swan,
With confidence and poise.
As dainty as a ladybird,
She never makes a noise.
As elegant as a model,
With mystic eyes that draw you in.
So angelic, an innocent beauty,
To dislike her is a sin.
She leaps and glides, as if a bird,
And once you've seen her, you are lured.

If you were to glance at her,
You'd *know* she was a dancer.

As agile as a kitten,
As languid as a cat.
Pointed feet in silken slippers,
One broken bone and that would be that.
Arabesque, plié, coupé
All made to look so easy.
Flexible from head to toe,
Polished, so you can say, 'That pleased me.'
Floating arms, carefully placed,
A gentle smile, upon her face.

If you were to glance at her,
You'd *know* she was a dancer.

Juliet Stirling (12)
Methodist College, Belfast

A Poem To You

When I'm upset,
And I'm feeling very down,
I know whom to turn to,
And it's you that can take away my frown

You are always there for me,
No matter what the time,
You always know what to say to me,
And you always let me know that you are mine

No matter what the topic,
You're always there for me,
Whether I'm in tears or not,
You always fill me with glee!

I only see you once a week,
And when Friday, I'm, oh, so very glad,
Running to the bus stop so I won't be late,
Transport these days just makes me so mad!

When youth club starts,
Everyone has so much fun,
You never leave me out not once,
We all have a laugh until the night is done!

When it's time for me to go home,
I feel so very sad,
You let me know you care with a hug
And I'll see you next week so it's not so bad!

Jonathan Tripathy (15)
Methodist College, Belfast

The Woods

The woods stand there, lonely,
beside the darkened stream,
standing during the morning fog,
unknown, like a dream.

No one dares to venture there
as they fear they won't come back,
so the woods just sit there, ignored,
with the lost and covered tracks.

One night as the sun went down,
that is when they came,
they cut down all the twisted trees,
no one thought it a shame.

Now the trees are gone,
and now the birds can soar,
where the trees used to be
and where they are no more.

Chris Carson (12)
Methodist College, Belfast

TV

TV is important,
Some people can't live without it.
They'll watch it day and night,
Unless they get a bite.

They come in shapes and sizes,
24 and 32.
You can watch it almost anywhere.
Even in the loo.

TV is important,
Though some programmes are a fright.
It is always best to watch them,
With a very bright light.

Brajith Srigengan (12)
Methodist College, Belfast

To Love Knotted

I would love you seven thousand years
And I would love you seven thousand more.
Yet from my love, my greatest fear's
That you'd not return my love in equal store.
From this fear my love is strangled,
And like Porphyria, preserved in time
In my fear, like hair, my love's entangled
To wait until your love calls out to mine.
'Absence makes the heart grow fonder',
Or does it weaken the heart's resolve?
And though I'd search, our lives are still asunder,
My love, like sugar in water, could soon dissolve.
And such a sweetness would be wasted,
For such a sweetness was never tasted.

Heather Murphy (16)
Methodist College, Belfast

Inevitable End

If you could be an oak tree I would turn
Into the leaves that hugged you day and night.
If you could be a candle I would burn
Above your head, exuding heat and light.
If you could be a painting I would choose
To paint you, hold you, frame you, love you too.
If you could be an apple I'd refuse
To be that which was not locked inside you.
Autumn comes: the leaves fall to the street,
With dawn the candle's flame exists no more.
The painting's to be sold to make ends meet,
What's left of the apple is rotten to the core.
I'm left with wistful memories of the past
As love, though good-intentioned, does not last.

Fiona Mulvenna (16)
Methodist College, Belfast

Spell Books

'You've waved your wand, and now you've cast your spell -
I never thought I'd feel such love for you.
But is this magic? I can never tell.
Still, these days no one loves you like I do.
It's unconditional; it's strong and true -
But I can't make you fall in love with me.
I've read the ancient spell books through and through,
With no luck . . . isn't that extraordinary?'
'Oh, don't you realise you could never be
A sunbeam in my sky of darkest black?
I'm flying high with someone else, and he
Has wings and hands and eyesight that you lack.
My magic's not for you, my foolish friend:
Your story won't be happy at the end.'

Ben Crothers (16)
Methodist College, Belfast

The Slowly Dying Flame

Love, the great betrayer:
A thin disguise for your lust
As your beating heart begins to rust.
Try to hold to the dream that you once believed:
Shut your mind to the world that you now perceive,
As you throw away all that you once held dear,
Your spirit held back by relentless fear -
Your fear of opening your eyes.
But deep within the dark recesses
Of my bleeding heart,
I peruse life's varied, bitter lessons
When life had yet to start.
For then I made the realisation -
Love and reality fall apart.

Eoghan Lavery (16)
Methodist College, Belfast

My Impressions

The quiet places are the best places,
Lonely, wild and free,
In the footsteps of Grace Darling, I'm travelling out to see,
The Farne Islands, tossed in a stormy, angry sea.

Haworth village in Bronté land,
Where forgotten, windswept trees,
Shade their rest,
Standing on this hilltop, a thousand miles I see.

Driving across Bodmin Moor,
Jamaica Inn in sight,
Looming greyly in the falling light.

Whitby Abbey, stark against the evening sky,
High above the sea,
At twilight waves quieten to a sigh,
Telling of persons long passed by.

I drove a boat to Innisfree,
Seeking solitude,
I found it there,
Life without care,
Lonely, wild and free.

Antonia McAlister (11)
Methodist College, Belfast

Even Now

Even now, I'm scraping mud off my boots,
It's light and warm and most men are sleeping,
Or playing cards, smoking or waiting.
The sun beats down brightly to dry my feet
Which haven't been dry for weeks, perhaps months,
The usual, in our muddy trench.

Even now, in the best kind of weather,
When the men have such a sense of good will,
I can't help thinking, it won't be long
Before it's dark and fireworks in the sky,
Would be beautiful if it weren't for the
Disgusting reality below.

Even now, in the peace of the daytime,
When there's comparatively little shooting,
And the men are sleeping or relaxed,
I cannot help but hear the sound of shells,
Bombs, rifles, shouting and high-pitched screams.
Perhaps it's in my head,
But the other men say they hear it too.

Lynn Hutchinson (16)
Methodist College, Belfast

Tiny Tim
(Based on 'I Have A Little Frog' by Anon)

I have a little puppy,
His name is Tiny Tim,
I put him in the bath,
To teach him how to swim . . .

He drank all the water,
He ate all the soap,
And now he's in his bed -
With bubbles down his throat!

Julie Forbes (11)
Omagh Academy, Omagh

World's Hope

I hear the rain tapping violently on the roof tiles,
I look out of the window, I see dull and despair for plenty of miles.
I think to myself *what the world was made for,*
And all that seems to come out of it is,
Suffering, violence and war.

Sitting on the same spot, watching people pass by,
I hear a burst of laughter but it turns to a sorrowful cry,
I think to myself *what the world was made for,*
And all that seems to come out of it is,
Suffering, violence and war.

Watching lives saved, seeing a baby just newly born,
Kids against violence and poor countries growing a feast of corn.
Peace talks and environmental campaigns
Perhaps the world is far more than just,
Suffering, violence and war!

Johanna Neary (14)
Omagh Academy, Omagh

Having Fun!

To have fun is to enjoy yourself, relax and unwind
To be free from all worries
To be free from all duties
And to spend time with all those you love.

It may be hard to find some free time
To try to relax and unwind
But when it is possible
You should spend the moments having a really good time.

Go out with your friends once in a while
Buy a drink, maybe two, if you don't mind
Don't be too uptight, relax and be kind
And have some fun for once in your life.

Christine Scott (15)
Omagh Academy, Omagh

Springer Spaniel

The warm glow of faith and trust,
Burns brightly in her eyes.
She's as protective as a mother,
And guards the house at night.

The speed she uses to hunt for me,
Comes from the snow leopards.
Whatever she does catch,
She brings home to you and shares.

The feel of her coat, so soft and smooth,
With a delicate touch to the skin,
Must have come from the smoothest blades of grass,
The colour of the white stone and the mud that she rolls in.

The pitter-patter of the rain,
As her paws touch the ground,
The grinding of boulder to corn,
To give her bark and growl.

A dog is a friend, a mate, a companion,
Someone to care for,
Someone to love
Someone to stay with evermore.

Zarah-Jayne Muldoon (11)
Omagh Academy, Omagh

Friends

F riends are forever. When you find the
R ight friend, they will always be a loyal and a true friend
I ndeed. They will stick by you in the good times and
E ven in the bad times. They will always keep a secret and
N ever tell anyone. They will always help you in times of
   need and you should never have to
D istrust them. Be glad to have a best friend.
S o if you don't, then go get one!

Naomi Deazley (13)
Omagh Academy, Omagh

Snow, Wind And Ice

Climbing wearily, must go on.
The harsh wind it does blow.
The blizzard I am lost in, will it ever let me go?
My hands are like ice,
My feet are like cement,
To my destination, will I ever get?
By now I'm barely alive,
My enthusiasm lost,
In the endless whirl of white candyfloss.
But somewhere a light still flickers.
Hope there is a trace.
To betray that now, would be an absolute disgrace.
So I trudge on grimly,
Hoping, forever hoping, trying to escape
From my snow blizzard prison filled with such unhappiness.
Till one day that beast calmed down.
I scanned my horizon all around.
My heart filled up with joy,
For then and there, I spotted my goal,
Just ahead was journey's end -
Where my slippers and blanket lay.
I smiled so hard that the evil cold went away,
My tears welled up in my eyes,
I beamed with such delight.
Oh yes! Home after a ten-year trek,
Over mountains, snow and ice.
All I want now is to go to my bed
And sleep and sleep and sleep
And sleep until my heart's content!

Alexandrina Todd (12)
Omagh Academy, Omagh

Winter

Winter is coming,
Winter is near.
Santa is humming,
With his reindeer.

Girls and boys,
Asleep in their beds.
Waiting for their toys,
And resting on their pillows,
Are their little heads.

The snow is white and cold,
With the Christmas tree up high.
The snow is soft to hold,
And soon Christmas will just die.

So we better make the most of it,
Before it disappears.
All my candles have been lit,
And now the sleigh bells are all
I can hear!

Emma Cummings (12)
Omagh Academy, Omagh

My Pets

I have a pet guinea pig,
And a rabbit that likes to dig,
The guinea pig lives in a box with the rabbit,
I have a Basset hound puppy,
Who wobbles when he walks,
He has very short legs,
And a long body,
He likes to sniff the rabbit,
And bark at the guinea pig,
My pets are very nice,
They are great!

James Riddell (11)
Omagh Academy, Omagh

What Ant?

I'm a type of ant
Who can go underwater and swim
I've seen the bottom of all rivers
But down at the bottom it's very dim.

I've got this long limb which is always in use
Oh, alright, I'll tell you, it's my nose
I use it to suck up my food
Now my poor tired mouth can close.

I'm the biggest of ants
Who pulls down trees
Just to make my home
And I'm an ant with four knees.

I've come to the end
I've just got one more clue
I'll spell my name with two 'E's'
And I'm a greyish blue.

Answer: An elephant

Naomi Browne (11)
Omagh Academy, Omagh

My Pet

Sparky is the name of my dog,
He is harmless, just like a log.
My dog is very fluffy,
But he is also very scruffy.

He likes to run around,
And roll along the ground.
In his sleep he growls
As if he is running after some owls.

He's got a little black nose,
With which he likes to smell a rose.
I love Sparky with all my heart,
I know for sure we will never part.

Rachel Leary (11)
Omagh Academy, Omagh

A Friend!

A friend is like a flower,
that never wilts away,
they're there when you feel lonely,
to brighten up your day.
A should for to cry on,
who never lets you down,
a friend you can depend on,
to take away a frown.

If ever you feel sad,
a friend is who to call,
they'll answer with a smile,
and talk you through it all.
Nothing's any trouble,
on them you can rely,
just ask them any favour,
and do their best, they'll try.

A friend will keep in touch,
no matter where you go,
on the phone they'll always be,
for you so well they know.
Wherever life does take you,
whoever, you do see,
the closest person in the world,
a friend to you will be.

Beverley Keys (15)
Omagh Academy, Omagh

Winter

W hite as paper,
 I n the garden.
N ever hot,
 T rees are covered.
E verywhere,
 R unning children.

John FitzGerald (11)
Omagh Academy, Omagh

Time Flies When You're Having Fun!

Charlene,
Going up town with her friends
And under the disco lights
Music, dancing and parties,
Time flies when you're having fun!

Simon,
Race cars, speedboats and surfing,
A ticket to Old Trafford,
'So little time so much to be done'
Time flies when you're having fun!

Anulika,
Working for hours in a field,
Under the Africa sun,
Disease, famine and war,
Yeah . . . time flies when you're having fun!

Cara McCarthy (14)
Omagh Academy, Omagh

The Last Goodbye

Standing there watching your eyes glisten,
You tried to speak but I wouldn't listen.
I turned away but you called me back,
I walked on, it was time to pack.

The next day came very fast,
I didn't want to make this month the past.
I looked down the airport and there you stood,
Hiding your tears under your navy hood.

You held me close and wouldn't let go,
Falling in love really has a low.
It was so hard to even try,
To give to you my last goodbye!

Vikki Lyttle (14)
Omagh Academy, Omagh

Hurt

I lie on the bed,
After slamming the door,
Thinking of the pain,
I've caused you before,
All over is hurting,
But I've hurt you much more,
All over a message,
Who could imagine such pain?
Just over and over and over again,
I don't know why I did it,
The reason was dumb,
It was a spur of the moment,
But it wasn't much fun,
I've hurt you before,
But never that big,
I think this is the last time,
We will ever be mates,
I apologise over,
It does no good,
I acted so stupid
Like I never thought I could,
Even think of those things,
I've never before,
It just came out,
But you didn't ignore,
The things that I said,
Even though they were lies,
I am totally self-centred,
And don't have a life,
I don't deserve to have one,
I'm just immature and dumb,
But enough about me,
This poem is pointless,
Just one reason I see,
As if you'll ever forgive me,
Just one tiny bit,
That's all I ask you,
But I've hurt you so much,
So it's hard to forgive me,

I don't know if I could,
If it was the other way round,
But you never could,
Say such stuff to me,
You're so gentle and nice,
It's just stupid lies,
That I said that to you,
Was evil, not nice,
I don't think I'll send this,
Even though I want to,
But I'm just so sorry,
That's all I can say.

Fional Crawford (15)
Omagh Academy, Omagh

Back To School

Back to school
Is not so cool,
Falling leaves and stormy gales
Autumn is approaching.
How many days are left to go
'Til Christmas time is here?
Winter's on the doorstep
And the season of good cheer!
Spring is round the corner
Now the winter chill is gone,
Gardens bursting into life
The start of a new dawn.
Summer's here, up goes a cheer
School is over for another year,
Holidays and summer sun
Guaranteed lots of fun.

Laura Fleming (15)
Omagh Academy, Omagh

Happiness Is . . .

Happiness is waking up on my birthday and finding a pile of presents.
Happiness is winning a hockey match.
Happiness is Friday at 3.30pm because it's the weekend.
Happiness is seeing a relative I have never seen before.
Happiness is going on holiday to somewhere foreign.
Happiness is listening to my favourite CD,
Happiness is getting a new mobile.
Happiness is getting a good result in a test.
Happiness is going to bed on a Friday night and not having
                              to wake up early the next day.
Happiness is chatting to my mates.
Happiness is shopping for clothes.
Happiness is watching my favourite video.

Lauren Alexander (13)
Omagh Academy, Omagh

What Is Wrong With This World?

People are dying
People are getting hurt in the street
What is wrong with this world?

Terrorism here and there
The terrorists are getting away with it
What is wrong with this world?

People being racist
Coloured people being hurt
What is wrong with this world?

I just don't understand these people
I don't understand why they do it
What is wrong with this world?

Alistair Barker (12)
Omagh Academy, Omagh

Loneliness Is . . .

Loneliness is running laps in PE and no one is near you.
Loneliness is getting picked last for a game.
Loneliness is being the last leaf on a tree.
Loneliness is lying on a hospital bed all alone.
Loneliness is having to play football alone.
Loneliness is being an only child.
Loneliness is doing detention by yourself.
Loneliness is sitting on a bus and you've missed your stop.
Loneliness is being singled out by a teacher.
Loneliness is a Manchester United fan surrounded by
                                          Liverpool supporters.
Loneliness is walking off as the 'Weakest Link'.

John Porter (12)
Omagh Academy, Omagh

The Arable Cycle

The yellow giants engulf the golden swathes,
Which yesterday danced in the breeze.
Next, tractors and balers condense the straw
Into uniform squares,
While the grain is blown into tall towers,
Ready for winter feed.

Plough blades glisten in the sun,
As they turn the brown earth up,
Preparing the soil for the seed.
Crows and seagulls hover overhead,
To catch the worms as they surface.
Soon the driller is at work,
Burying the seeds to start the cycle again.

Danny Millar (13)
Omagh Academy, Omagh

School - Or - Bed?

What is this buzzing in my head?
The alarm clock's screaming, 'Get out of bed!'
'Shut up!' I yell to the alarm
Ten more minutes will do no harm.

I lie and think about my day
Year assembly with Mr Hey
And all the subjects I detest
Like maths and French and all the rest.

Music and art are not too bad
But English really drives me mad
I pull the covers over my head
I've made the choice, I'll stay in bed!

Philip Hutchinson (12)
Omagh Academy, Omagh

You

I stop and stare
And you are there
My heart's desire
Is lit on fire

When I think of you
I think of the tulips covered in dew
Up in the mountain range
I never want you to change

I think about you every day
I never want you to go away.

Nikita Edgar (11)
Omagh Academy, Omagh

Happiness Is . . .

Happiness is going to a sleepover,
Happiness is going to watch your favourite football team and
watch them win,
Happiness is seeing the Christmas lights being switched on,
Happiness is seeing the glow on your sister's face when
she meets Santa,
Happiness is going on your second date (the first is
too nerve-racking!)
Happiness is holding a fluffy white kitten in your arms,
Happiness is lying on a lilo in the pool in Spain,
Happiness is opening your birthday presents,
Happiness is spending Christmas Day with extended family,
Happiness is watching the fireworks on Hallowe'en,
Happiness is scarce in the world today, enjoy it!

Jessica Keys (12)
Omagh Academy, Omagh

Football

In life it is my sole ambition,
To play football in the tradition
Of my father,
To me he is a sporting great,
He's taught me to appreciate,
The finer points of the greatest game,
Which may never lead to instant fame,
But to me it's life, it's love, it's passion,
It's football!

David Fulton (14)
Omagh Academy, Omagh

I Am Who I Am

Today we judge people on what they wear,
Their shape or religion and colour of their hair.
The size that we are matters very much,
Or even how much we eat for dinner or lunch.
If we have glasses or the colour of our skin,
The shape of our bodies, are they fat or thin?

The colour of our eyes, the shape of our head,
All of this should seldom be said.
But this doesn't stop us, you see,
Because the person we are is not who we want to be,
And although we don't have a clue,
These things are being said all around you.

Rachel Giles (12)
Omagh Academy, Omagh

Autumn

The leaves have all turned brown,
And are lying on the ground,
It's autumn,
The hard work has all been done,
The harvest has been won,
It's autumn,
The sun's rays have grown dim,
The nights are closing in,
It's autumn,
Soon the weather will get chillier,
And the fires are all lit earlier,
Now it's *winter!*

Christopher McAuley (13)
Omagh Academy, Omagh

A Knock Around The Head

When I was playing rugby I got a slap around the head.
When I got home I went straight to bed.
Now when my mother heard about my knock,
she got quite a shock.
'Now this will not do,' she said,
'for my boy to get a knock around the head.'

My mother wasn't happy when I said I was oh, so sleepy.
She said, 'This is no time for napping,
when you got such a slapping around the head.
'I'm afraid you'll have to go and see the doc
after such a knock!'

Richard Vaughan (15)
Omagh Academy, Omagh

The Woodland Creatures

The little robin redbreast, you see him from time to time
In amongst the branches, or in-between the twine.
Sitting in the flowers, or soaring through the air.
The little robin redbreast brings happiness and care.

The little grey-furred squirrel, sitting in a tree,
Gathering acorns in groups of two or three.
Hiding them till winter, when everything goes bare.
The little grey-furred squirrel brings happiness and care.

All the woodland creatures from deer to small dormice
Waiting for the winter snow, and the cold, cold ice.
Soon they will awaken, in their woody lair.
All the woodland creatures bring happiness and care.

Susan Wilson
Omagh Academy, Omagh

Spring

Spring is my favourite time of year
When the sky is not dull but clear
New baby chicks are born
Running around looking for corn
New lambs are brought into the farms
Flowers are blooming like wonderful charms
When spring is over I am very sad,
But when next year comes I will be glad.

Alexandra Sproule (11)
Omagh Academy, Omagh

Cromwell Street

Something wrong at No 25
Body after body, corpse after corpse
As the police were told prose after prose
About the horrific lives of evil Fred and Rose.

A mother whose daughter is missing
Is praying and hoping her daughter is listening
She hopes, she hopes, as her heart still beats
That her daughter is not among the dead at
Cromwell Street.

The house is knocked down but the horror remains
The house is ripped apart but there's still a broken heart
The place where nine bodies once lay
Is now just a lonely path where the sunshine rays
It's still there
The lonely, desolated
Cromwell Street!

Robert Giles (14)
Omagh High School, Omagh

At Hallowe'en

Hallowe'en can be quite fun
It can also be quite scary
Goblins, ghouls, witches and warlocks
And werewolves that are hairy.

> Every year at Hallowe'en
> I'm as pathetic as can be
> With my plastic mask and bin liner cloak
> That my mum gave me for free.

When we go out trick or treating
People often ask
Has my face always been that ugly
Or is it just a mask?

> I try to be original
> But never get it right
> Would you be scared of a bin liner
> Even when it's night?

But next year I'll show them all
I'll be the scariest thing in town
I'll dress up as my mother
And wear a dressing gown!

Daniel McGaughey (13)
St Joseph's High School, Omagh

Pets

My favourite pet is a little, white cat.
My worst pet is a big, black rat.

My little cat is called Tina
She loves to play with Leana

Leana is the cat that lives next door
Who loves to lie all day and snore.

Tina loves to eat soft creamy rice
Leana likes to eat fat, juicy mice.

Tina chases Penny, the dog
Leana loves to run around the bog.

Tina is very active
But Leana is attractive.

I play with Tina all day and night
In fact - I don't let her out of my sight.

Tina has sharp, long claws
Tucked nicely in beneath her paws.

Tina was born on the 1st of May
In fact I think that was a wonderful day!

As Tina, Leana and Penny march up the stairs
They jump into bed and say their prayers.

I love to kiss Tina goodnight *but* . . .
It's not worth my while when she gives me a bite!

Anne-Marie Devine (11)
St Joseph's High School, Omagh

Sweets

Sweets, sweets, sweets
Everyone thinks sweets are neat
Every kind of sweets
So chewy, just like meat
Snickers, Crunchies, bars galore
Thinking of these makes me want more!

Crunchy, chewy, hard and sticky
I love sweets so much I'm not picky
Crisps, ice cream and wriggly worms
When you bite in they are stiff and firm.
I chew and chew till my mouth gets sore.
After eating these I want more!

Mars, Drifter, and many more.
I'll eat sweets till my stomach gets sore
Mint, chocolate, sugar and powder
The smell of these are like a flower
Sugar tastes and feels so good.
Sweets really are my favourite food.

Amanda Hood (11)
St Joseph's High School, Omagh

Save Our World

Stop polluting our world
Or there will be nothing left
For our children's children,

Nothing,
Emptiness.

All the water will be polluted,
All the animals will die,
The air will stink
There will be no life on Earth,
Our countryside will be in ruins,
Empty.

If we all work together
We can make a difference
Recycle our rubbish, use unleaded petrol,

Bring our empty bottle banks.
This will make our world a better place.

Ciaran Browne (11)
St Joseph's High School, Omagh

The Future

I often wonder what the future will be like,
Will cars have three wheels
With tyres that have spikes?
What will the future be like?

Will trees grow down
Instead of up?
Will flowers smell bad and trees smell nice?
What will the future be like?

Will animals roam the Earth?
Elephants will be pink,
Well, that's what I think,
What will the future be like?

I often ponder,
On what will it be like?
Will the Earth be the same?
Oh, what will change?

Ciara Campbell (11)
St Patrick's Academy, Dungannon

My Dream

Let me tell you about my dream
I have no idea what it might mean
Now, close your eyes and picture this scene . . .

A group of men dressed in red and white
Another group in orange, what a sight!
All this was taking place in broad daylight.

Up and down a pitch they ran
Gaining points appeared to be the plan.
All in aid of some Cup called Sam.

There was a crowd there to roar
After each miss and score
Some said they had got in using the back door.

At last a whistle blew
And onto the pitch some of the people flew
Congratulating Mickey, Peter, Eoin . . .
To name but a few.

When I awoke
My mother had just spoke,
Saying, 'Have you wet that bed
After drinking too much Coke?'

Megan Kelly (11)
St Patrick's Academy, Dungannon

My Likes And Dislikes

He loves to sit upon my knee,
One day I thought I saw a flea.
Cats.
I love them.

They look so colourful and so sweet,
I sometimes get them as a treat.
Flowers.
I love them.

It pounds upon the windowpane,
And very often floods the drain.
Rain.
I hate that stuff.

You clean and wipe and scrub the floors,
It makes you stay all day indoors.
Chores,
I hate them.

Roseanna Weech (11)
St Patrick's Academy, Dungannon

The Willow On The Water

Like a ghost mirrors its late vessel,
Dulling colour and the form,
The water echoes the willow tree,
As from reality it's torn.

No longer true, but distorted,
As ripples lace the plane.
The colours fuse and agitate,
Diminishing as of rain.

When all is still as prior,
No displacement to be seen,
Another realm is perceived behind,
The surface where no one's been.

The leaves are moulded together,
And only hue defines,
The shape and texture of the tree,
Because all else combines.

A breath of wind causes a stir,
A swift downpour of foliage,
Around the blemished verge they land,
And decorate the image.

The firmament, bright and blue,
Forms a blurry bound,
Around the willow, and makes a scene,
Consummate and sound.

Tara Mullin (14)
St Patrick's Academy, Dungannon

Enlightenment

My humble feet have travelled
All through the wretched night
I have wandered through cliffs
And thought of my ever-ending life.
I have heard the sullen quietness
And felt the bitter cold,
My heavy head finds no rest
Finding answers to all my struggles,
Tortures and troubles.

For hours I have
Overlooked the rough, rowdy sea
Numb and feelingless,
Day by day the tough city life has drained
What was once warmth.

But as I lie in darkness
Far away from the noise and distraction
A light has shred through the dead landscape.
The horizon heals all the misery
And gives me an unexplainable new hope.

I will live now
Because life is a blessing to each of us
Who is lucky enough to have it.
I felt lost and was suddenly found.
And to envisage such beauty
In my dull heart
Will let me forever capture
The everlasting mystery of life in nature.

Breda O'Kane (15)
St Patrick's Academy, Dungannon

Flowers

Dancing in the breeze,
The vibrant colours exploding from their core,
The petals' cushiony softness waiting for a bee to come to rest,
Their cherub-like centres smiling at the sun.

So delicate and beautiful in their attire,
Warming the cockles of my heart,
Their sweet aroma glides elegantly through the air,
I am filled with wonder and awe.

A giant sunflower reflecting upon the glowing fireball in the sky,
A red rosebud erupting like a volcano,
A mass of white lilies like a fall of snow,
A breathtaking experience.

Wild and free they grow,
Watching nature around them,
Bursting open,
I am filled with wonder and awe.

Catherine Wylie (15)
St Patrick's Academy, Dungannon

Hallowe'en

Hallowe'en is here this year
To fill you full of horrifying fear
It gets scarier and scarier year in and year out
It's that hair-raising experience, you want to scream and shout!
Keep close to your friend and be careful that night
Because you never know who's out to give you a fright!
There are monsters, ghosts, witches and beasts.
They all meet up for midnight feasts.
Then they leave in search of some more meat
So watch out little children, on your *'trick or treat'!*

Clare Martin (13)
Sacred Heart College, Omagh

Hallowe'en

Oh, Hallowe'en, how I'll scream,
When phantoms come in that team,
Barking, howling and haunting me,
No grannies saying, 'Come in for tea.'

Knocking, knocking at my door,
For goodness sake, my head's now sore,
Phantoms at my door now retire,
Yes, finally I can go and light my bonfire.

Flames of the bonfires way up high,
Fireworks are flashing, colouring and lighting the sky,
A cut, designed and fiery pumpkin,
Everyone laughing, scaring and drinking with kin.

The children come home, bags full of sweets,
Running around the bonfire eating treats,
Everyone all snug now in bed,
There's nobody now to wake the dead.

The ghoulies and the phantoms all go home,
Back to the land of Hallos Dome,
I've got so much to say,
All about one Hallows day!

Eliza Harvey (12)
Sacred Heart College, Omagh

Oh What A Night!

It was a dark night,
Oh, what a fright!
The wind was very sharp
Like a discordance harp.
The trees were shaking
As the men were raking,
So out came the evil
Of that night,
Oh, what a terrifying,
Bone-shaking night!

Sabrina McKenna (13)
Sacred Heart College, Omagh

It's Taken A Long Time To Get Here

Red and orange with a touch of blue,
A sea of anxious and hopeful faces,
Waiting for their heroes to burst upon the scene,
'It's taken a long time to get here!'

I pray that Tyrone warms up at our end,
My prayer goes unanswered.
The screen is my only hope for a close-up of my heroes,
'It's taken a long time to get here.'

The whistle blows, the match commences,
The talking is over, the work begins,
In seventy minutes, we'll get our answer.
'It's taken a long time to get here.'

Canavan's frees, Cavanagh's miss,
Hearty's save and McGuigan's dummy.
It's going well but it's not over "til the fat lady sings',
'It's taken a long time to get here.'

Second half, but where's Peter?
Gotta have faith, gotta have faith.
Captain's gone, O'Neill's on,
'It's taken a long time to get here.'

Mulligan's miss, Gormley's block,
Marsden's off, Canavan's on,
It's watch-checking, nail-biting and heart-thumping time,
'It's taken a long time to get here.'

'It's taken a long time to get here,'
Announced Peter as he triumphantly raised *'Sam'*,
Past defeats fade from memory,
It was worth the wait!

Aáron Grugan (13)
Sacred Heart College, Omagh

My Hero, Roy Keane

You're one of those players,
You either love or hate,
But to me, personally,
I think you're great.

You might not be that tall,
But you are great on the ball.
For Man United you're number sixteen,
And you're known as the 'mean machine'.

When you played for Ireland,
You wore your jersey with pride.
And you would still be doing so,
If McCarthy hadn't lied.

When you were sent home from Japan
The fat really hit the fan.
Some say you're too hot-headed and you reacted too quick,
Because you didn't listen to Big Mick.

They say you are a loner,
And you are as thick as champ.
But I respect you because you listened to your head,
Even though, it broke your heart.

Keane, you are the leader of the pack,
And when you play,
Your team never lack.
You are miles ahead of the rest,
And to me personally,
I think you're the best!

Mark Garrity (13)
Sacred Heart College, Omagh

What Am I?

As red as the setting summer sun
As white as the fallen fluffy snow
I hear a noise as deafening as a rocket blasting to space
And see warriors running on a green carpet
As swiftly as a flying Ferrari
A round white sphere as fast as a shot from a cannon
Travels between two poles
Long and thin like signposts to the sky
At last a bowl like a shining chalice is held up high
Faces as happy as a million birthdays and Christmases.
What am I?

Croke Park on All Ireland Day!

Cathy Davis (12)
Sacred Heart College, Omagh

Hallowe'en

Children are getting ready to trick or treat
Eating toffee apples
That are very sweet
'Can we let off some fireworks?' the boys and girls ask their dads.
'OK, OK, just stop asking, you're driving me mad.'

See the fireworks blast like a rocket up to the sky
The babies wake up and start to cry
The dogs bark
What a noise!
The parents call in their girls and boys
They are very tired but have lots of sweets
Next year is another year to trick or treat.

Taylor Lowe (12)
Sacred Heart College, Omagh

Untitled

For the first time ever
Tyrone have Sam Maguire,
We have to admit against Armagh,
They were on fire.
To play for the winning team is every footballer's desire.

Peter Canavan played great,
He's as quick as lightning,
When he hurt his foot, it was frightening,
He can kick with the left and the right,
In every match he puts up a good fight,
He isn't a messer with the ball,
He can kick an over from almost anywhere at all,
Taking shots, he misses never.

There's also Brian Dooher,
Although he's quite small
He picks up all the breaking balls,
He is a big threat,
Did you know he's a vet?

Then there's Owen Mulligan
The woman's man,
His hair is bright,
He's as quick as a ray of light.

Don't forget Ryan McMenamin,
He's certainly not slow,
As we all know,
Without him the team will never grow.

Daniel Gorman (12)
Sacred Heart College, Omagh

Hallowe'en Night

On every Hallowe'en night,
We all dress up
Some people look quite a sight,
Of course there are others as sick as a pup.

They say they've seen the witch,
Flying through the skies all night
And cackling in the ditch,
But they were never right.

I found out the witch's name is Wendy,
She wears netty tights
Her broomstick is very bendy,
But she tries to fly with all her might.

She hasn't got a friend,
That wants to laugh and play
So all Wendy does is sit in her den,
Through the whole day.

When Hallowe'en is over,
Wendy goes away
In her little Rover,
All the way to Lusty Bay.

Lauren McCarron (13)
Sacred Heart College, Omagh

Toys

What would toys do at night?
Would they have little tea parties at midnight?
Would they walk about as if it were day
Or would they show the little ones how to play?
Or would they gossip about one another,
And maybe they would get into bother?
Or would they just sit every day,
Listen to us and what we have to say?

Kerrianne Clarke (13)
Sacred Heart College, Omagh

Twins

My twin sisters, they are very annoying
When I go shopping all I hear is
'No, Mum, she can have our clothes.'
But I know there is going to be a change
Because they are growing up,
Moving out and going to new places
So then I don't have to look at their annoying faces.
Even when Mum meets her friends
All they talk about is 'twins'
'Twins, what did you get in your exams?'
'Twins, do you remember . . .?'
But when I go to tell my mum,
It's always a case of jealousy!
And I know myself, it's not
So please when you meet me
Do not talk to me about twins
Because all they do is confuse me.

Karen McMahon (13)
Sacred Heart College, Omagh

My Favourite Football Team

They are green and white
Their defence is tight
When other teams play them they feel sick
My favourite football team is Celtic.

In midfield there's Thompson and Agathe
Thompson's as strong as an ox and as quick as a cat
When Agathe outruns someone, it makes them look a bit thick
My favourite football team is Celtic.

Up front there's Larsson and there's Sutton
Larsson is my hero and Sutton's shots are like bullets from a gun
When Larsson leaves at the end of the season, I'll probably cry
But my love for Celtic Football Club will never die.

Barry Kerrigan (13)
Sacred Heart College, Omagh

The All-Ireland Final 2003

I can't wait for the weekend to start,
I may even see the famous Mickey Harte,
It will be so exciting,
I hope there is no fighting.

Finally Saturday has arrived,
We are packed up and ready to drive,
On the way down it is fun,
And I really hope Tyrone do win.

At last, Sunday is here,
I am in such great fear,
We make our way to the pitch,
All that walking gives me a stitch.

The players are finally out,
We all scream and shout,
The ball has been thrown in the air,
I just stop and stare.

Half-time is here,
I am still in fear,
Tyrone is doing very well,
As we can all tell!

The players are back out,
Again, everyone shouts,
The ball has been thrown for the catch,
We know we need to win this match.

Two minutes are just left to be played,
As the commentator has just said,
This is all so tense,
I can't wait to jump over the fence.

Oh my goodness, that's the final whistle,
My toe is sore like walking on a thistle,
This is like a dream
Just to see the team.

Peter walks up,
To collect the cup,
We all scream and cheer,
And we will be back again next year!

Aisling McAleer (13)
Sacred Heart College, Omagh

The Rally

The lights are green,
the wheels turn,
making a yelping sound.
The car shows
its need for speed.
It turns the corner,
the clock is on,
the car is heaving,
the wheels are pulling,
it burns round.
There is only one place
where it is bound . . .
the ditch!
We listen for the engine
but not a sound!

The axel is bent up in a 'V' shape
for everybody to plainly see.
The clutch has fallen out.
The driver shouts, 'The car is out,'
but still they shout.
The driver gets out,
the clock is stopped,
the wheels have popped.
It's all over!

James Keenan (12)
Sacred Heart College, Omagh

The Kitchen's Gone Crazy!

The taps keep dripping,
The pipes have sprung a leak,
There's no water for the dishwasher,
There's no washing for a week.

The saucepan lids keep rattling,
The spoons have got the shakes,
The carving knife keeps buzzing,
The oven won't bake the cakes.

The microwave keeps *pinging,*
The light goes on and off,
The kettle keeps on boiling,
And that's with them both turned off.

The cupboard doors keep banging,
The shelves jump up and down,
With packets, jars and tins and things,
My mum's brought home from town.

The fridge and freezer are getting hot,
They must have blown a fuse,
The iron pumps out smoke not steam,
There's nothing safe to use.

Dearbhla Byrne (14)
Sacred Heart College, Omagh

Hallowe'en

Hallowe'en is now this time of year,
With dressing up in ugly gear,
With painted faces and unusual masks,
And trick or treat is the task.
Bonfires are set alight, fireworks are shining bright,
As people gather in a crowd, the ghost stories shall begin
Of what had happened to the young and old.

Emma McCullagh (12)
Sacred Heart College, Omagh

Tyrone's Return

The night was lit,
With balloons and beer.
And the crowd would cheer,
Every time they heard 'Tyrone' in their ear.

The crowds were gathering,
It was all such a fuss.
And the thousands went wild,
When they saw Tyrone on the bus.

The party went on for hours and hours,
The crowds climbed high,
As high as some towers.

Alas, alas,
It had to come to an end
And people went stumbling
Back home to their bed.

Matthew McKenna (12)
Sacred Heart College, Omagh

Loneliness

I'm all alone,
Isolated,
No one beside me,
No one to talk to,
No sound,
No voices,
No light; dark night,
It feels like it will end,
Too scared to speak,
Too scared to sleep,
I'm all alone,
Isolated!

Aine Morris (15)
Sacred Heart College, Omagh

Moon And Stars

Stars
In the middle of the night,
I look up and see some lights,
Stars are smiling back at me,
Smiling back with all their glee.
They are little but have such might,
Shining brightly in the night,
Like countless diamonds in a mine
Like a web of fireflies on a pine.
They are little but can't you see
They have more power than you or me.

Moon
I see a man sitting on the moon
Looking down at us, wondering *what's the fuss?*
They build a big rocketship to blast them off to space,
But the journey is made to be quite a waste.
Sure, they get some rocks and stones
But they don't find my real home.
You may think that I live all alone, on this big moon on my own . . .
But as usual you've thought wrong again,
Come and see, the answer's plain.

Maeve Brogan (12)
Sacred Heart College, Omagh

Time Alone

I will be the gladdest thing under the sun,
I will touch a thousand flowers but will never pick one,
I will look at hills and the sky with wondering eyes,
And then watch the wind blow on the grass
              and see the grass wave goodbyes.
People will then start to show up from the town,
And yet when I see them coming, I don't want to come down.

Joanne McGoldrick (12)
Sacred Heart College, Omagh

Omaha Beach

Thirty seconds till we get to land,
The shelling is non-stop, people say we won't survive,
Now I wish I was in a pub listening to an Irish folk band,
Once the door opens, some men will be slaughtered like lambs.

The boat door is open, 'It's time to go!'
I shout to my platoon to 'Stay low!'
There is a flood of bullets, all different sizes,
But, too late, the men have started their cries.

Soldiers, white as ghosts in their sleep,
Blood stains the sand like a luxury carpet,
It's like a giant leap into another world,
Now I wish I was with my friend in the local market.

People yell with agony and pain,
Body parts lying around the beach,
The medics trying to keep the broken-hearted soldier tame,
We need the German fort breached.

Some of my platoon and I have reached the bank,
The platoon argue over what to do,
Then I look up and see something like a tank,
A mighty blast comes from it and I go into a dream.

My body feels very strange and sore,
All I can think about is my family,
All I can see are my comrades on the German fort floor,
It feels like my family is slipping away from me.

I can't see anything, it's like I'm in the dark,
I wake up and I see white,
Then I know it is the end of my flight.

Conor Rafferty (13)
Sacred Heart College, Omagh

William 'The Braveheart' Wallace

William Wallace, he was brave
His country from England he tried to save.
He fought the noblemen to the end
And his beliefs did not bend.

His goal was simple and so true
He knew exactly what he had to do.
He gathered an army to fight the fight
To give Scotland back her true birthright.

They fought with everything they had
But things started going bad.
William was captured and led away
Would he live to fight another day?

Sadly it was not to be
They tortured him to death, you see,
But before he went to the Lord's kingdom,

William's last words were for Scotland
'Freedom!'

Kieran McCullagh (12)
Sacred Heart College, Omagh

The Greatest

My favourite hero is Roy Keane
He's angry and mean
Now playing for the Red Devils
Up along with the two Nevilles
More medals on his rack
Will soon give Alex a heart attack
Getting older every day
Soon will leave the job to John O'Shea
Squad number 16
The unstoppable Roy Keane!

Matthew Walsh (13)
Sacred Heart College, Omagh

My Grandad

My grandad is the best man,
That I have ever come across,
He might be starting to get old,
But I don't care, he's as good as gold,
He takes me here and takes me there,
And wherever I want to go.
I don't know what I'd do without him,
He's so good to me,
You would never know.
He buys me this and buys me that,
And anything I want.
I wish, I wish he'll always be here,
Because when he's gone, I'll just sink,
                          into deep despair,
For when my grandad
Is not there!

Rebecca McDonagh (12)
Sacred Heart College, Omagh

A Typical Day

As my mum opens the door,
I hear a bunch of keys
Rattling in her pocket.
In she comes
And sits down to have a rest.
I hear the phone ring
And the door knock.
I go and answer the door
And in comes my brother,
As my mum talks on the phone about her day,
I hear the laughs and shouts down the phone.
She puts down the phone
And yawns and sighs,
As she drifts off to sleep,
The silence fill the house.

Kerrie Sharkey (11)
Sacred Heart College, Omagh

The Evening

It's the evening, 5pm, Mum makes the dinner while
I sit and do my homework. The fan of the cooker
makes a breezy sound while the food is cooking.

You can hear the music from the living room,
coming from the TV. I sit on the kitchen table
listening to it while I do my homework.

I can hear a car outside and see the trees
moving in the wind, but can't hear the wind.

The table is covered with some of my books and
my sister's books, she is doing her reading and
speaking out loud and my mum is now helping her.

I have now finished my homework and I wait
for another evening like this evening.

Roisin McGovern (11)
Sacred Heart College, Omagh

Weather

Rain, rain is such a pain
I wish I were in sunny Spain
Pitter-patter on the windowpane,
I see the rain coming down like a train.

Sun, sun is lots of fun
It makes me want to skip and run,
Oh how I wish that I were cool,
Jumping in a swimming pool.

Snow, snow is very white
It makes the world look very bright
I wrap up warm when I go out,
To stop Jack Frost when he's about.

Eamie Gormley (12)
Sacred Heart College, Omagh

The Atmosphere In The Classroom

Well, what can I say?
The teacher's up and about,
And she has great doubt
The work isn't good,
We're all thinking of food.
It's Monday morning,
And everyone is tired and moody.
All they want to do,
Is to go back to their beds.
Some days the kids are happy and cheery,
And other days they are sad and lazy.
They love the days without homework.
They just hope the classroom
Is a happier place tomorrow.

Ciara Morris
Sacred Heart College, Omagh

My Old School

The old school sits and moans in the dark,
Alone and forlorn, there's no one around,
Mice can be seen scurrying around the stairs,
Isn't it a pity that no one cares for its repairs?

Sometimes I can still hear the children
Laughing and playing,
But that was long ago I fear,
That was another day.
The school's jolly times have gone
But it's not a crime, it's served its time.

Barry McGinn (11)
Sacred Heart College, Omagh

Summer Days

Summer days are so hot,
Children at school don't have to be taught!
Getting up later, be an angel or sinner.

Breathing fresh air,
Not playing fair,
It doesn't matter what you do,
You can stay out till half-past two!

Dreaming about going back to school,
Cinema, play park and the swimming pool.

Girls and boys going on holidays,
The 'sun' is shining always.

Football, dodge ball and basketball,
The trees are standing high and tall,
The flowers are blooming,
The cars are zooming.

Summer days are just the best.
Summer days beat the rest!

Aisling Dolan (13)
Sacred Heart College, Omagh

Do You Want A Witch's Power?

Do you want a witch's power
To put a spell on your granny?
Or to make your teacher's sums go wrong?
Or to turn your dog into King Kong?
To make yourself invisible
Or to make your enemies disappear?

But first you will have to find a witch,
Which will not be an easy job, and
Even if you do, they will not give up without a fight
So good luck to you, if you want a witch's powers!

Conor Moore (13)
Sacred Heart College, Omagh

In And Outside The Classroom

A dog barks outside,
I hear the stream of cars,
Going down the new motorway,
A teacher opens the door,
Remembering me, that I am in school.

The trees brushed by the wind,
The dog barks again
I hear people's desks creaking,
A workman shouting outside
Saying, 'What will I do with this?'

The teacher corrects the work,
The noise of the pen
Scribbling on the paper.
With her pen marking away,
She turns to the next page.

Outside the classroom,
Doors open and creak,
Teachers walking down the corridor,
The heels of their shoes
Clicking and *clicking* as they fade away.

Martin McGoldrick (12)
Sacred Heart College, Omagh

Sport

Sport, sport what a sweat
Sometimes you get wet
Sport, sport the thing to do
Even if you have the flu.

Sport, sport hockey, Gaelic and football
Sport, sport hurling and baseball
Sport, sport is for all ages
Sport, sport you will gain some wages.

Jonathan Browne (13)
Sacred Heart College, Omagh

The School Corridor

The school corridor is very long and colourful.
The children are hard at work in their classes.
The bell will ring soon.
There, the bell has rung.
Children rushing out of classes to go to break.
Mr McDermott's coming out of his office.
Sweet papers on the ground,
Jimmy's lifting them up.
The bell is ringing to go to class,
Teachers telling pupils to hurry up.
Now the corridor is quiet and clean again.
The children are in class again.
The pupils cannot wait for dinnertime, then home time . . .
Jimmy the caretaker is brushing up the corridor again.
Teachers saying, 'See you all on Monday!'

Cathal McGuire (12)
Sacred Heart College, Omagh

School

The sound of people's pens
Scribbling in their books,
Dogs barking at nearby cars,
Endless traffic going on and on.

The doors squeaking as teachers go past,
Deliveries being made,
People whispering amongst each other,
The wind blowing and whispering.

The sound of the teacher opening drawers
The teacher sorting out books,
The sound of people packing their books away,
The sound of people leaving the classroom.

Darren Mullan (13)
Sacred Heart College, Omagh

The Flu!

When I was in school one day,
I felt a bit sick,
So I asked the teacher
Could I go to the nurse.
The nurse asked me what was wrong,
I said I had a sore stomach
With a sore head too.
She said to me that I had only one thing,
I asked her what was this thing.
She replied, 'The flu!'
I wondered what was this
And what it could do.
I felt all weak and tired,
So I must have had the flu.
The flu, I found out
Is a common thing
In the cold weather.
In this condition I wasn't able to sing.

Hugh Colton (13)
Sacred Heart College, Omagh

School

School, school, what a bore!
Please, please, show me the door!
Homework nearly every night
Oh what a horrible fright!
If you don't do your homework you're in trouble
The teacher's gonna burst your bubble!
The bell rings at the end of class,
Time is quickly flying past,
Twenty past three, time to flee!
I rush back home, happy as can be.

Christopher Colton (13)
Sacred Heart College, Omagh

Loneliness

What is it like to be lonely?
It can lead to sadness and depression
Going through a long, long day
Loneliness can bring out in people the worst
Fill them with rage, anger and aggression
Leave minds all over the place, filled with confusion
To be alone, to be alone is a curse
It's like being in a dark room, tight with little spaces
No one there with you
But memories coming back, bringing you happy faces
In your chest, your heart is weeping
Locked in a cage
With good memories it's keeping
To be alone, to be all alone
Nothing to watch, no one to phone
The only company you have, is your own
To be on your own, what's the point in life?
It hurts the mind and the heart
Like a stabbing from a knife
You're all alone, on your own
No kids, husband or wife
The saddest thing is, it could last forever
Forever mourning, tears make the river
Drowning your sorrow, in the cold water you shiver
To cry and weep, is all you've known
And it many never change
Destined forever, to be all alone.

Kieran Colton (15)
Sacred Heart College, Omagh

Tyrone Deserved Sam And They Got It!

A dream come true
And not only for me
But for the whole of the county of Tyrone
Especially the players!

Nail-biting, heart-stopping seventy-odd minutes
And I was there
The excitement was unreal
Unbelievable, ecstatic and very emotional.

When the final whistle blew,
I was speechless
We'd won an 'All Ireland'
I felt *so* proud to be born and reared in *Tyrone!*

The journey back was some craic!
Although there was almost gridlock in some towns,
With cars bumper to bumper,
Blaring horns and vibrant decoration,
A sea of red and white,
Traffic or tiredness didn't seem to matter!

The next day, the parties began
When the team travelled round
And thanked and praised everyone
For their support and encouragement.

The players have trained hard
Not just this year but for a long time
Their effort and commitment has paid off
And now they have got what they have worked hard for -
> *The Sam Maguire Cup!*

Orla Clarke (14)
Sacred Heart College, Omagh

Loneliness

I feel like no one loves me,
Does anybody care?
Will someone stay beside me?
Is anybody there?

At night when all is dark,
In silence, I'm on my own,
Can't get to sleep for ages,
When I know I'm all alone,

I need someone to listen,
Will someone come hold me?
I need to escape this loneliness,
Will you set me free?

A feeling of cold inside,
And still I can't see,
Who's going to comfort,
Care and chat with me?

Roisin Quinn (14)
Sacred Heart College, Omagh

Loneliness

It's silent,
   quiet,
     there's not a sound!

It's dark,
   lonely,
     and there's no one to be found.

Searching!
Searching!
Trying to find,
A person, a home, a love, I want
For my own!

Laura Garrity (14)
Sacred Heart College, Omagh

A Leafy Day

I woke up on that
leafy Saturday morning
I quickly
put on my clothes
I dashed outside like a bird in the sky
I swam through the leaves
and I climbed up a tree so high
and
dashed into a pile of leaves
and as I
laughed and played
on that
cold autumn day,
I was
so
happy to be alive
I was so
cold I could hardly breathe
the cloud from my breath
was all around me
just as it was for Daisy our cow.

Niamh Goodwin (11)
Sacred Heart College, Omagh

Loneliness

Silence, emptiness and gloom,
Is all that fills the room,
Afraid, unwanted and alone,
Has she got a heart of stone?

Sadness, tears and pain,
Oh what is there to gain?
Isolation, loneliness and fear,
Where are those she once held dear?

Louise Kelly (14)
Sacred Heart College, Omagh

Peace And Quiet

Sitting here in English the classroom is quiet,
Everybody's working hard,
I listen very carefully as the peace is soothing,
I can hear cars on the road and a dog barking.

Looking round I can see heads to the books,
Concentrating on what to do next,
Somebody searches for a pen, the peace is broken,
I look round again.

The peace is back for now,
The dog is still barking
And the cars are still driving,
What to do next?

Waiting for the bell takes forever,
My teacher's reading a pupil's work,
Me staring round to see if no one's working,
But still the class is quiet.

As heads bend over white pages,
Scratching pens in the hope for inspiration.

Helena Kirwan (12)
Sacred Heart College, Omagh

The Blue Whale

I am in a boat out in the sea,
Something jumps up out of the water,
Oh, what could it be?
I rush over driving the boat,
It is a giant blue whale, it looks frail.
I call the local coast guard to see if it is all right,
It looks to me that it has been in another fight.
The coast guard comes out,
The blue whale is away,
It jumps in the sunset hoping it will come back another day.

Eamonn McGovern (12)
Sacred Heart College, Omagh

In My Classroom

In the room I am sitting now I hear,
the traffic out on the busy road,
dogs bark and people roar.

Teachers coming in and out,
I just wonder what it's all about,
police coming into the office,
someone's been caught scheming or stealing
or maybe there's been a break-in?

Work, work, work, work, that's all we ever do in school
the sounds of the day
the background noise for the work.

The sharp voice in the corridor,
a door bangs
a phone rings
cars blowing their horns
windows close
the music blares from the music room
Jimmy, the caretaker, with the brush.
The principal goes to get a phone call
people chat
people's footsteps click along
vice principal talking to a teacher.

Then a bell rings and class is over
till then next class, to see what else we can hear.

Bernadette Nugent (12)
Sacred Heart College, Omagh

A Poem About School

In the Sacred Heart College
I enjoy it so much
my friends do too
and I can't stop doing that much

The school principal is Mr McDermott
is very good too
but he can be very cross sometimes
and can be in a very bad mood

In the corridors
you hear the pupils talk
and when they come to school
they always do a walk

Outside you hear noises
trees and cars and lorries
and when you do something bad
you always want to say sorry

My daddy is a youth tutor
he works very well indeed
he is the best I think
and gives me everything I need

My brother Conor McMahon
he does help me so
he is very bad sometimes
and sometimes is very slow

Mr McKenna is very good indeed
he is a very strong man
and that is what you need
and he sometimes has a can

The school is very good
the pupils and staff
are always very kind to me
and are never that daft

The relatives of our family
they are very kind indeed
some of them come to SHC
and they really are a good need

My sister Marian McMahon
used to come to St Brigid's
she didn't like school at all
and I think she was a right idiot.

Eamonn McMahon (11)
Sacred Heart College, Omagh

The Day Sam Came Home

Sam came home on Sunday,
We all couldn't wait to see,
The team in their uniform
As happy as can be.

Sam arrived at a quarter-past ten,
The cheers from the crowd were loud,
The bands were playing, the drums were rolling,
The voice blasted from the microphone for all to see,
Our wonderful cup, our son Sam, back home in Tyrone!

Mickey Harte's men had done it!
The army in red and white
Fought against Armagh to show
That the Co of Tyrone were always right.

We were right because we knew we would win,
All the signs, all the efforts to support Tyrone were all good
And they worked,
Because Sam is home in Tyrone.

Allana McMenamin (12)
Sacred Heart College, Omagh

Every Sound

The lorry and cars driving along the road,
The sound of a cross dog,
The noise of the people writing a story,
The noise of a door opening.

Again the dog barks,
The caretaker's cleaning and delivering things,
The voice of a teacher roaring at a student,
The sound of people breathing.

The noise of people played PE,
Shouting, 'Pass, pass, I'm free!'
The dog is getting cross again,
The noise of the teacher blowing a whistle.

The noise of a teacher opening boxes,
The sound of a closing door,
The click of heels of shoes,
The sound of crunching up boxes.

Gerald McAleer (12)
Sacred Heart College, Omagh

My Noisy Brother

My brother's such a noisy kid
When he eats soup, he slurps.
When he drinks milk, he gargles
And after meals he burps.

He cracks his knuckles when he's bored
He whistles when he walks
He snaps his fingers when he sings
And when he's mad, he squawks.

At night my brother snores so loud
It sounds just like a riot
Even when he sleeps
My noisy brother isn't quiet!

Shane Mullin (14)
Sacred Heart College, Omagh

The Weekend

Finally it's Friday, it's half past three,
The bell rings, now we are free!
I set off home for the night ahead,
Because it won't be late till I'm in bed.

Now it's Saturday, the best day of all,
Go up to Derry to a big shopping mall.
I'll buy some clothes and maybe a phone,
At the end of the day there'll not be a moan.

Now comes Sunday,
The day before school,
How boring will this be?
I'll call in with the flu.

I'll pack my bags
And get my diary signed,
Goodbye weekend,
Hello school!

Ruairi McGinn (13)
Sacred Heart College, Omagh

Feelings

The room goes quiet, not a sound to be heard
The pale blue sky, no sign of a bird
The trees are swaying back and forward
The autumn is near and the sound of the song bird
Fills your ears with a sweet, gentle tune
Sadly I won't hear it all as I have to go soon.

The bell rings, the bird stops singing
The phone starts to ring, a constant ringing
The noise rises in the corridor as pupils come from every direction,
The everyday life makes me sigh with affection.

Now it is my turn to take my leave
The emotion goes and I am filled with grief.

Aisling Meenagh (12)
Sacred Heart College, Omagh

Yesterday It Happened

Yesterday it happened in school,
It was so cool,
We went to the pool.

And when we got changed,
We went through the showers,
I felt like a flower getting watered.

While I was swimming,
I felt my tummy turning,
I started swimming away.

When I got out,
My friends started to shout,
'Are you feeling okay Shauna?'

When we got back,
We started to unpack,
And we wanted to go back.

My hair was soaking,
I'm not joking,
I am hoping
It won't be long till we're back.

Shauna Murphy (12)
Sacred Heart College, Omagh

Friday, Last Period

It's last period at last, at last,
Can't wait to get out the school doors.
Looking out the window sadly,
See the leaves falling down onto the ground,
Hear the wind blowing in my ears,
Oh, how I wish to get out now!

There goes the bell at last, at last!
I go to meet my friend Terri,
We run down the hill as happy as can be,
Finally I can say, that's another week over for me.

Erin McGuigan (13)
Sacred Heart College, Omagh

Outside My Classroom

Outside my classroom you can hear everything,
People talking,
Dogs barking,
Footsteps,
Jimmy lifting rubbish,
John with his brush,
Mrs McCusker with her photocopies,
Everyone's in a rush,
Parents coming in to collect their son or daughter,
Police coming, they've caught someone scheming,
Mr McDermott walking quickly to his office for a phone call,
The classroom assistant hurries to get the girl she looks after,
Here comes Jimmy again,
Now he has got the mop,
The dog is still barking,
And the cars never stop,
This is what you can hear from Mrs Madden's English room
(Room 1.)

Sarah Owens (12)
Sacred Heart College, Omagh

Travis, The Angel Dog

Travis is my dog,
We play all day long,
We go for walks in the park mostly every day,
He is a Dalmatian, but not a spotty one,
We wash him every Saturday,
And then we give him a treat,
Travis is pampered and loved,
He is nice, cute and sparkly,
We've had him for three years,
And those three years were magical,
I'd never be fit to take it, if he starts to be an angel.

Mairéad Quinn (11)
Sacred Heart College, Omagh

Wake Up

In my bed lovely and warm,
All tucked up sound asleep,
Dreaming, dreaming pleasant thoughts,
Then an alarm goes off, too cosy to get up,
'Please, another five minutes!' I beg.
I doze off again and then
I heard my mother shout, 'Are you ready?'
Quickly I sit up in bed,
She'll kill me for not having stirred.
I hear her footsteps angry and loud,
Pull on my blouse and skirt,
Which I lift from the floor,
Crumpled a *little,*
But what does it matter?
The heat from my body
Will soon iron them out.
'Up yet dear?' Mum enquires.
'Of course Mum,' I reply.

Emma McCarroll (13)
Sacred Heart College, Omagh

Summer Morning

One summer morning
at the break of dawn
a pretty little doggy
came walking up the lawn.

A lovely coat
of white and brown
and a curly tail
that went round and round.

Two big eyes
so full of glee
oh that little doggy
looked so happy.

Keri-Anne Donnell (11)
Sacred Heart College, Omagh

As We Are Being Told Off Again

As we are being told off
Our teacher silently reads the work of children
She picks up her pen and is speedily marking the papers.

As we are being told off
Someone walks through the classroom door
And her voice turned from a shout into a conversation whisper.

As we are being told off
People walk past the door and stupidly stop to look in
After being seen they vanish and run for their classroom.

As we are being told off
The caretaker comes into the class with a pile of boxes
When the teacher turns to thank him the noise of the children
Has risen again.

As we are being told off
The children at the back of the room drift into a daydream
While the people at the front can just sit back and be shouted at.

As we are being told off
She writes letters to the parents of misbehaving children
Suddenly the bell goes and we leave knowing that we have
only one day until it starts all over again.

Christopher Ruddock (12)
Sacred Heart College, Omagh